Starving SEASON

ONE PERSON'S STORY

Seang M. Seng MD

Lulu Publishing Services rev. date: 8/10/2017

Dedications

To father and mother

I know I've not done enough to give back for all the lifelong lessons you taught. Thank you for accepting me for what I am and for giving me the chance to go to medical school. Thank you for doing your very best to protect our family during "the starving season." You're no longer here with me, but we meet often in my dreams. You always stressed the importance of education, and I have passed this on to your grandchildren.

Srey

I asked you to follow me, and you did. Thank you for your courage and for having faith in me, and thank you for raising our children to be the best they can be.

To my children--I love you all.

Sakona, you are the oldest, born and raised at the time I was poor, consumed with school and early career. I missed many of your school activities, especially basketball games. In spite of this, you showed me you could grow up on your own. I am very proud of you for becoming very independent early in life.

Kosal, you were predicted by your classmates to be the most successful person of your class, and I agree with that. I see great potential in you and I cannot wait to see what you will become.

Sakara, you have lived the most colorful life of all. You are sweet, obedient, and caring, and for this I thank you.

To Daniel Susott

It's hard to believe that 35 years have passed since we met. You gave me the chance to start a new life, a lifelong gift that affects not only my wife and me, but our three children as well. I thank you from the bottom of my heart.

To America

While in the refugee camp, I was offered a chance to resettle in France, but I was willing to wait for America. I picked America and became a citizen as soon as I could. I made the right choice. Thank you, America.

Acknowledgement

To my editor: Craig Stevaux

Over 30 years ago, you told me you were willing to edit my book if I ever wrote one. Today I thank you for the many hours you spent editing my original manuscript. Without your diligent work, this book would not have come out the way it has.

Thank you.

Preface

Nobel Peace Prize Laureate Elie Wiesel, in "Night," writes,

> For the survivor who chooses to testify, it is clear: his duty is to bear witness for the dead and for the living. He has no right to deprive future generations of a past that belongs to our collective memory. To forget would be not only dangerous but offensive; to forget the dead would be akin to killing them a second time.

It wasn't until after I'd escaped the killing fields that I seriously thought about writing a book. Before that, the thought had never occurred to me. And the reason was simple: I had no story to tell. My early childhood was no different from the majority of other Cambodian children I knew--I played barefoot in the yard and ran around naked with friends when the monsoon rains arrived. My later childhood was mainly the life of the average kid whose primary job (outside of school), like almost everyone else in the neighborhood, was to help out his parents. Once I was old enough, I pedaled an old bicycle to deliver merchandise my father sold from his grocery--charcoal, rice, soda, and other items--to customers' homes. Though I later attended medical school (the first of my family to do so), thousands of others before me had attended the same school. There was just nothing special about me.

History changed that.

* * *

If I had to describe a primary characteristic of Cambodian people, I would say it is the smile. This isn't just my personal observation. Long before I was born, the Cambodian smile was evident in our ancestors' carvings of smiling Cambodian faces and the smiling faces of the graceful, dancing Apsara that adorn the walls of Angkor Wat.

Never would I have dreamed that one day our Cambodian people (called the Khmer) would trade their smiling character for a brutal, ferocious face that killed countless of their own.

The Communist movement in Cambodia began in the 1940s. Khmer students living in Paris organized their own communist movement, separate from the French Communist Party. The notorious Pol Pot, then known as Saloth Sar, joined the party sometime between 1949 and 1951.

Growing up, I lived in a country that Prince Norodom Sihanouk termed an "island of peace." Prince Sihanouk, however, had allowed North Vietnam to use the eastern part of Cambodia as a sanctuary for troops transiting the supply network known as the Ho Chi Minh Trail. Though Cambodia existed as a neutral country, President Nixon and Henry Kissinger, desperate to cut the North Vietnamese line of supply, initiated a secret bombing campaign inside Cambodia. Under the saturation bombing, an unknown number of villagers' lives were lost. These ferocious attacks forced many Cambodian villagers to either flee the countryside to seek refuge in the capital or join the Khmer Rouge.

In 1970, the neutralist Prince Sihanouk, who had managed to keep the nation out of the war in neighboring Vietnam and the entanglements of Laos was overthrown in a coup by General Lon Nol. The Cambodian civil war raged for the next five years. During this period, nearly all agricultural infrastructure was destroyed, and the nation went from being self-sufficient in rice production to being dependent on foreign food aid.

The Lon Nol government fell to the Khmer Rouge in April 1975 when the Khmer Rouge occupied Phnom Penh, by then a city swollen with internally-displaced persons. The Khmer Rouge immediately evacuated the capital, forcing everyone to go to work in labor camps in the countryside. Families were often separated and sent to different locations.

* * *

I began writing a story when I was in the Khao I Dang refugee camp on the Thai border more than 35 years ago. At that time, my intent was only to tell readers what the killing fields looked like--nothing more. I knew I was among the few who had survived the massacres and starvation, and thought it should be an interesting book--a general look at life under communism, but not necessarily a personal story. I never completed that story, however, because I had other things to ponder: surviving the refugee camp, looking for sponsors to help me and my wife get out of the camp, all the while counting our chances of relocating to a third country. My dream of authorship turned out to be short-lived. I didn't speak English well enough; nor did I have the time and patience to accomplish it. This couldn't be my priority at that time. Still, even during the struggle to build a new life with a new language in a strange land, the thought of writing a book remained with me.

My son, Sakona, was born only ten days after my wife and I landed in Honolulu, Hawaii. I went to high school to take GED classes, worked at a variety of jobs here and there, finally attended college, and, ultimately, medical school. Time was not on my side, and now many years have passed.

But the passage of years doesn't necessarily mean time lost. Now I have a larger story to tell. This book isn't just a general story about life in the killing fields. Although one of millions, it's *my* story. It's about *my* struggles in the labor camps, how I survived the killing fields and made my way to a refugee camp, the friendships I made there with the American volunteers, particularly members of the American Refugee Committee (ARC), and how I struggled to survive in America.

* * *

Historians say some 1.7 million people lost their lives in the Cambodian Holocaust, though the exact number will never be known. Whenever I try to tell someone about my misfortune and tragedy, I always fear he or she won't believe me. If "the starving season" was that severe, how could I survive? If the killings were so widespread and targeted to intellectuals, then how is it that I, a Phnom Penh medical student, was missed?

Usually I don't share my story with people I don't know well, because I'm not sure they will take it to heart. Many years ago, a good friend, Dr. Daniel Susott, asked me if I would contribute a chapter to his book "Years of Horror, Days of Hope." My piece began with the word "death." It seems so much of my story involves death. For this, I am sorry. Regrettably, the memory of the Cambodian Holocaust has begun to fade from our collective memory. I write this story down as my daughter has so often urged me to do--*my* story--so that my children and grandchildren will grow to understand where and *when* they came from.

All that matters about *my* personal story is that I lost everyone in my family. In 1975, our family of 24 persons was trucked into the countryside and trudged into the killing fields: mother and father, my five sisters and me, my grandparents, my uncle's family, my mother's siblings, and my sister's family.

Four years later, I hiked out of the killing fields alone.

Chapter 1

Thankfully, it wasn't raining. August was nearly the peak of the Southwest Monsoon, and I don't know what we would have done if it were raining. The thirteen Chinese open-bed military trucks that made up our convoy were packed with people standing shoulder to shoulder under the dull-eyed gaze of the men in black with AK-47s. For the most part, the Khmer Rouge were friendly, but firm. Distant, but polite. They didn't talk a lot, mostly just to issue us instructions. When they did speak, they called us "*Pok Meh,*" for father or mother, or else "*mit,*" which means comrade. There was no place to sit in the truck, so I stood at the very back. I started to think of what life would be like without any real home. *Or destiny.* The civil war was over, and I reasoned it would take time for the new government to get us all settled. From my spot at the back of the truck, I wanted to see how Phnom Penh had changed in the four months since we'd been driven out of it.[1]

Even before the war had swelled it with soldiers and refugees, Phnom Penh boasted a population of some 600,000. By 1975, the capital city had swelled to nearly two million. But now I looked out at a ghost town; all the doors of the houses and shops were closed and every building was empty, even along Monireth Boulevard. Our sad line of trucks moved through deserted streets. Except for the sight of an occasional military truck, I saw nothing else move. No bicycles. No mopeds. No cars. And, except for a few scattered soldiers, I hardly saw any people.

Our truck rolled along past the Olympic stadium that was built when I was in elementary school. The government had built this immense stadium right next door to my school, Bak Touk. I remembered the racket the rocks made as they passed through a grinding device, reducing them to small stones. In 1966, our Prince Sihanouk had hosted a visit by French President Charles de Gaulle. I was a 15-year-old ninth grader then and proud to be

---

[1] Phnom means "hill" or "mountain" in Khmer. Penh is a woman's name.

1

selected for the youth choir. Each student had been chosen to perform for the French president, if only to carry batons or sit in the stadium with colored panels which, when flipped, produced giant portraits of President de Gaulle or Prince Sihanouk. To welcome the French President to the newly completed stadium, our youth choir sang La Marseillaise, the French national anthem. The 50,000-seat stadium was packed with people. I'd never seen such an extravaganza, and I was part of it! In his speech that day, President de Gaulle guaranteed the neutrality of Cambodia. From my childhood into my adult years, I lived in a country Prince Sihanouk had coined the "island of peace." And that was true. Outside our borders, wars raged in Vietnam and Laos, but we continued to live in peace. That is--until the civil war.

As the truck continued on, we jounced and swayed. It turned down Jawaharlal Nehru, then to Confederation de la Russie to Preach Monivong Boulevard. Once on Monivong Boulevard, I could see the Royal Railway Station. Once a very busy station, this day it stood empty and silent.

Across from the station was the Buddhist stupa that housed relics of the Buddha. It was constructed following Cambodia's independence from the French. During the Buddhist religious festival called "Visak Bochea," thousands upon thousands would gather here to celebrate and remember Buddha's birth, enlightenment, and death.

Beside the stupa was my medical school, the place where fellow students and I used to play ping pong all night long in the cafeteria on those occasions when we were assigned to "guard" the facility against the Khmer Rouge. Now, it, too, sat empty. The front stairway where we used to congregate was empty. No professors' cars were parked in front. No scooters, mopeds, or bicycles were parked at the side.

Next to my school was the largest cathedral in the capital. This area was home to a French community: the French Lycée, the Lycée Descartes, the Cercle Sportive, and the famous "Le Royal Hotel," temporary home to Jacqueline Kennedy during her 1967 visit. All now deserted.

At the end of Monivong Boulevard stood the French Embassy. Empty.

I saw that the bridge allowing people to cross to the other side of the Tonle Sap River was empty, its middle portion destroyed by the Khmer Rouge in order to cut the government's supply line during the war.

Crowded together in the back of the truck, we talked quietly with each other. I saw no fear in people's eyes, but everyone tried to guess where the dour figures in black would take us. Of course, it was only rumors passing from person to person like butterflies flitting from blossom to blossom. No one knew for sure where we were being taken. *Or what would happen to us.* Some of the elderly people began to repeat an old Buddhist prediction that our country would go through a time when "there will be houses where no one lives; there will be streets where no one walks." This was predicted many years ago, they said. They also said we would face starvation so severe that "we would eat a grain of rice that stuck to the dog's tail." We might even know what they called "the land of the pregnant men." I had no idea what they were talking about. The city around us was totally deserted, true enough, but our family still had food reserves. We weren't starving. I had never heard of such nonsense. *They must just be making this up.*

We turned onto Highway 5 that paralleled the Tonle Sap River to our right, and then, only 12 kilometers outside Phnom Penh, the caravan of trucks passed through my birthplace, Prek Pnov. But now, I could hardly recognize it. It, too, was a ghost town, no different from the other villages we'd passed through. The market that teemed with people every day of the week was now lifeless. For as long as I could remember, Prek Pnov had been a bustling transit point. All the buses travelling from Phnom Penh to the west of the country would stop here. In those early days, the rickety yellow or green buses lined up on the south side of the market, their roofs piled high with travelers' luggage or merchandise. Scores of travelers milled about the buses in search of this or that coach. Child vendors hawking merchandise piled atop their heads called out to the bus passengers. All sorts of fruits from mangoes to star fruit to fried and roasted bananas passed up through the open bus windows to passengers' outstretched arms. Sticky rice sealed in bamboo stalks was a favorite as were small, sour melons sprinkled with salt and red pepper. Another was sugar cane that was peeled, cut into small pieces, and skewered on bamboo sticks. Vendors soaked the cane in ice buckets to keep it fresh and cool. Plastic bags of cane juice and soda dangled like colorful water balloons from the hands of child vendors. Flies buzzed everything. Bus horns blared from everywhere warning passengers either to clear the area or hurry up and board as the drivers yelled out the next destination to be sure passengers were catching the right bus. The ground beside the buses was both loud and peaceful at the same time as vendors plied their trade and black smoke belched from the exhausts of departing coaches.

I saw that my elementary school, the school I'd attended for a year as a youngster, stood abandoned. When I was young, I used to walk in my school uniform of short-sleeved white shirt and blue shorts along this very road. Students who lived farther away pedaled to school on bicycles. There was no school beyond our elementary school in Prek Pnov so all the students were very young. Every school day, this road was filled with laughing, noisy children in the morning and afternoon. Next to the school was a brick factory, one of the largest in the vicinity. Each day, countless numbers of massive trucks rumbled out of the yard, hauling bricks to Phnom Penh and elsewhere. Now, it too, stood silent and empty.

My birth village was the place where people stained clothes black by using dye from a fruit called "macleu." By Cambodian tradition, elderly women wear the *sampoot*, a robe similar to a sarong and always black. Before the war, rows upon rows of these black garments lined the ground beside the road. But now, there were none to be seen. Gone, too, was the pungent smell of fish sauce made here. In the old days, whenever you passed Prek Pnov, you couldn't miss this other cottage industry, a trademark of my village, the strong smell of rotten fish.

It's custom in Cambodia to assist thirsty travelers so we place a large ceramic urn of water and dipper in front of our houses so that passing strangers can avail themselves of a cool drink, but now, all along the road, the houses and water vessels were all empty. There was hardly anyone to be seen. I asked myself where all the people were.

From time to time the trucks stopped, and the Khmer Rouge allowed us to get off but only to relieve ourselves--beside the road for men and deeper in the bushes for women. Otherwise, we were to remain on the trucks. My eyes sought out the small brick signs on the road that were built by the French when Cambodia was one of its colonies. These indicators were the few things that were certain, telling us how far we were from the city. The only other clue we had to our location was the occasional provincial or village sign. I knew we were headed northwest, but I wasn't familiar with this road at all. It was National Highway 5 that stretched from Cambodia's capital, Phnom Penh, and ran all the way to the Khmer-Thai border.

* * *

After a trip of more than six hours from Kampong Kantuot, somewhere between Pursat and Battambang provinces, our truck finally came to a stop. There was no other traffic on the road. By the sun's height in the sky, I could tell it was late afternoon when we were ordered to get out. This time we were told to take all of our belongings. Each of us carried a few changes of clothes, a mosquito net, a blanket, and the *krama*, the traditional Khmer checkered scarf. Others climbing down from the truck had hidden jewelry and other valuables in their underwear. One man had concealed valuables inside a bamboo cane. As for me, I'd tried to hide as much as I could in my red karate uniform bag. When we were forced from our home, I'd grabbed my emergency kit stuffed with medications and various instruments I'd collected from the hospital over a period of time during the war.

The Khmer Rouge ordered us to stand on the left side of the roadway until all the trucks had arrived and all the passengers were off. Even though we were a crowd, each of us felt alone standing on the side of Highway 5. Mother had told me--"Wherever we go, we go together"--so my job was to make sure our family didn't get separated. My sister, Sy, had two children, the youngest only a few months old, and her boy, Vimol, was four. My youngest sister was twelve, old enough to take care of herself. My mother and the rest of the family made sure that Sy got as much help as she needed. We felt sorry for her--having to take care of her two children by herself since her husband had been taken away a few weeks before.

There was no sign of a village or old town in this area. No one lived here. We could see a dirt road heading toward the forest, but we didn't know where it led. Once the other trucks had arrived and all of us were offloaded like so much cattle, a few black-clad Khmer Rouge ordered us to start walking along the dirt road. We were frightened of what might happen next, but we could do nothing but follow their instructions.

Whatever it was, fate or karma, we were all slaves now. We'd been trucked like livestock from our temporary place in Kampong Kantuot through Phnom Penh and into the western part of Cambodia. We had no idea where we were and no idea of what lay ahead of us. As what remained of our family shuffled along the dirt road, my Uncle Chin Huot held to his conviction. In both Phnom Penh and Kampong Kantuot he'd convinced the family that the evacuation was only temporary. Now he predicted we'd be allowed to return home in six months, but I didn't think so. An uneasy feeling had seized me that we would probably be here for a long time.

Whatever was in store for us, I was sure we weren't going home any time soon.

Chapter 2

Though I was raised in a family that practiced Buddhism, the religion of nearly the whole population of Cambodia, I was never a strong believer in any religion or faith. I couldn't remember the last time I ever prayed for anything except to pass my school exams.

In Cambodia, the educational system was modeled on the French with its national exams. When I was a young boy, before I took any national exam my mother would ask me to be "blessed by the spirit." My mother, Sochou, was born into a family of twelve children, though three died young. Among her surviving four sisters and four brothers was one brother, Uncle Chin Hor, who was my own age, and so we were in the same grade in school. Before each of these general exams, the two of us were instructed to sit on the floor with our legs to the side (the polite way to sit whenever we listened to Buddhist monks chanting at the temple). We lowered our heads, closed our eyes, and raised our clasped hands in prayer; this is what Cambodians call sompeah, *a gesture of both greeting and submission. Grandpa would recite a Buddhist chant aloud. I'd heard this many times, but after the Buddhist chant he also recited in a strange language, one I never understood.*

Suddenly, there would come a loud clap! Grandpa had slapped both thighs with his hands. He was now in a trance; no longer was he Grandpa. A spirit had entered his body, and the spirit would proceed to sprinkle us with water, wishing us good luck on our exams. My family taught me to believe in this, and, for a time, I did. After all, Chin Hor and I always passed our exams.

* * *

By April 1975, my fourth year of medical school, I was 24 years old. I volunteered to work in Monivong Hospital, the main military hospital in Phnom Penh. I took special pride in working here because another of my uncles, Nay Heng (my mother's younger brother and the first member of our family to attend medical school), had rotated through this hospital before me. In fact, it was Uncle Heng who introduced me to Monivong Hospital. Uncle Nay Heng joined the country's military very early in his medical school career and planned to become a surgeon, the same career I dreamed of. He was my role model. He shared the same trim and wiry frame as Chin Hor and I possessed, but unlike Chin Hor and me, he wasn't particularly interested in sports. Or music. Even during the Beatles era he wore his hair short (though he loved to wear dark glasses in a rectangular frame). As far as I was concerned, he was the smartest of the family and the one I always turned to for advice--so much so that I became his shadow, following him everywhere. He seemed to enjoy my company, too. He patiently tutored me in algebra and geometry, two subjects with which I really needed help. In those days, a student could receive two diplomas--one from a Khmer school and a second called "Brevet" presented by a French school, the Lycée Descartes. This was the French national diploma, but you had to excel in French in order to pass this test. Nay Heng earned high honors in both; I tried to emulate his achievement, but my French wasn't good enough. Uncle Nay Heng loved to attend the Cine Lux, the only major theater in Phnom Penh that offered French movies, and I frequently tagged along. I admired him for his impeccable French; he would translate the movie for me even as we watched it.

In 1973, when he was in his fourth year of medical school with two years left before graduation, Nay Heng joined friends for the medical school's annual end-of-year ball, the biggest and best party in the city. Most of the students attended. The organizers always arranged for well-known performers or a famous orchestra, and that year's "Ball Medecine" featured a well-known female singer, Mao Sareth, who performed her famous song "Dark Black Sky." A few weeks later, several of us got together with Uncle Nay Heng and friends at Arey Ksach, a small island located across from the palace. Chin Hor was there with his girlfriend. I was there too, but we didn't dare tell our parents or grandparents. They expected us to focus on our studies; school wasn't supposed to be fun. Both Nay Heng and Chin Hor knew how to swim though the water surrounding the island was shallow enough that we could wade in and out without fear. Uncle Nay Heng went out into the water while Chin Hor and I stayed on the island. Sometime during the evening, Nay Heng disappeared suddenly. His body wasn't found until the next morning.

* * *

It was quite rewarding for me to be able to help the wounded soldiers at Monivong Hospital, and though I wasn't a surgeon yet, I hoped to become one. My role model at that time was Dr. Khun Song Soeung. Known as one of the best surgeons in the country, his signature dress was his white suit. He never wore anything but white and always ironed it to military code. The pleats were always perfect, and, though he was an authority figure, he always flashed a charming smile. He'd received his medical training in Paris, and I'd heard he even taught anatomy there before returning to Cambodia. He taught us anatomy in our second year of medical school. What an artist! All the bones he drew on the blackboard were as perfect as the ones found in the anatomy text. The humerus and the ulna bones of the arm, for instance, always looked to be in perfect proportion to each other. I never wanted to see him erase any of his illustrations. They were simply too beautiful. He knew all the muscle insertions, arteries, veins, and nerves off the top of his head. He used colored chalk to highlight different parts of the anatomy--red for the muscles, yellow for the nerves, and so on. As a student, I had a very hard time trying to keep up. Staying attentive to his lectures while at the same time struggling to copy his exquisite drawings into my notebook was next to impossible. What a figure he presented as he strode back and forth, pausing to draw on the chalkboard--a dazzling figure in crisp white as he created art for his students!

Dr. Soeung was greatly admired for one of his heroic acts: he risked his own life to remove an unexploded M79 bullet lodged in the armpit of a soldier's wife. The woman had been shot by the Khmer Rouge in the village of Peam Roh. For everyone's safety, the site of the operation was moved outside to the hospital grounds. A crowd gathered at the perimeter to watch as the patient was placed in a thick metal box designed by the hospital staff. The box had two holes on Dr. Soeung's side and another small hole on the top so he could place one eye to see the patient during the operation. On the box's opposite side were two holes for the assistant to Dr. Soeung. Dr. Soeung proceeded to remove the oversized bullet using his left hand so that in the event the munition exploded he would lose only that hand. After some tense moments, he succeeded in removing the bullet. Afterwards, he placed it in a hole that had been dug on the grounds. Later, it would be detonated by military personnel. The patient was transported back to the operating room to close the incision. In the end, no explosion ripped through the hospital grounds that day.[2]

Since the beginning of 1975, Cambodia's U.S.-supported military government controlled only the Phnom Penh area and a string of towns along the Mekong River that provided the crucial supply route for food and munitions coming upriver from South Vietnam.[3]

With the war approaching closer and closer to the city, the medical school had closed weeks earlier. Our capital of two million people was being slowly strangled. Everyone knew this day would come; we just didn't know when. Although Phnom Penh hadn't yet fallen to the Communists, chaos gripped the city. Shelling had become a daily occurrence, and grenades seemed to be exploding everywhere in the city, particularly in the cinemas. Many people took shelter in Buddhist temples. Our family

---

[2] As the nation descended into chaos and killing, Doctor Soeung refused to flee even though he was given the opportunity. He was killed by the Khmer Rouge soon after the communists took over the country.

[3] In March 1969, the U.S. began secretly carpet-bombing eastern Cambodia. The Ho Chi Minh Trail, a network of pathways from North Vietnam extended through Laos and Cambodia into South Vietnam. As American war involvement escalated, this trail system moved deeper into Cambodia. The B-52 bomber flight records of attacks on neutral Cambodia would be falsified by the American commander in Saigon, Gen. Creighton Abrams. As bombers returned from missions over neutral Cambodia, two sets of reports were filed--one true, the other false. Between March 1969 and August 1973, the United States dropped 2,756,727 tons of bombs on Cambodia.

was one of many who'd dug a trench in our yard to jump into in case the shelling got too close.

The Khmer Rouge was always looking for ways to disrupt life in the city. They didn't care about the lives of civilians; all they cared about was winning the war no matter the cost. They even planted grenades in movie theaters to kill innocent people. I never thought this barbarism would persist after they took over the country. I thought once they'd won, the killings would stop.

By April 1975, Monivong Hospital was inundated with wounded government soldiers. As large as the hospital was, it wasn't large enough to accommodate the increasing number of military casualties. Patients were everywhere. They filled the hospital's beds; they lay on the floors, even on the walkways, just everywhere. Their uniforms were torn and covered in blood. With soldiers being admitted to the hospital outnumbering those leaving, there wasn't even time for sanitation. Tile floors became slippery with blood. Because the main operating rooms were reserved for the more serious cases, minor surgeries were performed on the patients' beds and even on the floors--anywhere we could find an open space. I loved to assist in these cases because I wanted to be a good surgeon. Between cases, I visited post-op patients so I learned quite a bit as to who did well and who didn't. By this time, with such an impossible daily workload, we as medical students just looked around and, based on our gut feelings, decided which cases we could handle. Some of the fifth- and sixth-year medical students were forced to become surgeons, leaving only the more complicated cases to the attending physicians. Often, I didn't like doing cases outside the operating rooms because there was no teaching, and I had to do them by myself. I did well enough with easy cases like the removal of shrapnel from under the skin that didn't involve large vessels. As a medical student, it was nearly impossible to find an attending physician. They were just too busy in the main operating rooms, which ran day and night.

I remember one soldier who was brought in with a lacerated trachea; I was afraid to touch him, knowing full well that I'd never so much as assisted with a tracheal repair, let alone performed the surgery by myself. That day, I turned to my attending physician who just said, "Sew him up. You can do it." I worked nonstop every day, and I was on duty every other night. I spent less and less time with my family. I was exhausted, but I loved every minute of it.

On April 16, 1975, I was on duty at the hospital. For some time, we'd expected the Khmer Rouge to enter Phnom Penh. They'd been inching closer and closer to the city. Huge flames could be seen climbing into the western sky from a gas station that was only six kilometers distant. On the first of April, the Khmer Rouge overran Neak Luong, the last remaining government resupply point on the Mekong River. On the same day, General and Premier Lon Nol resigned and left the country, a sure sign that the war against the Khmer Rouge was lost.[4] On April 12, the U.S. Embassy was evacuated by helicopter. By the 16th, the shelling of the city reached such intensity that I didn't want to stay late at the hospital, I wanted to be at home with my family. I wanted to phone them, but couldn't. You had to be very rich to own a telephone, and the Seng family didn't have one, so I had an ambulance take me home.

The next day, April 17th, the Khmer Rouge entered the city. With the guerrillas' arrival, everybody--myself included--thought peace had finally come. Smaller groups of fighters entered the smaller streets. Groups of ten to twenty soldiers in black uniforms, their standard dress, marched through the main streets. They wore *krama*, the traditional Cambodian checkered scarf, on their heads and rubber sandals cut from car tires. Military trucks were filled with fighters. Some rode captured US-made armored vehicles. Along the roadsides, the crowd lined up many persons deep. City-dwellers ran into the street to shake their hands in welcome.

After years of warfare, propaganda, and speculation, we city dwellers were curious. Exactly who were these Khmer Rouge? We knew they were communists. Once known as the Communist Party of Kampuchea (CPK), Prince Sihanouk gave them the name "Khmer Rouge." But beyond changing our country to communism, what did they want? What would happen next? We even wondered what these fellow Cambodians looked like. The Khmer Rouge fighters we saw were all dark-skinned, giving us an

---

[4] President Nixon had immediately embraced the right-wing leader of the 1970 Cambodian coup, General Lon Nol. Nixon ordered the CIA to implement a plan for maximum assistance to Lon Nol who proclaimed himself President of the Khmer Republic.

impression that they were likely pure Khmers (without the mix of Chinese blood so many of us had) and probably farmers from remote parts of the country.[5] The Khmer Rouge were to take the name *Angkar*, a word which translates as "the organization." The Khmer Rouge we observed this day were all quite young, some no more than boys. Each fighter carried a gun, usually an AK-47 or M-16. Others carried pistols or grenade launchers. Yet some of these soldiers smiled and even appeared to welcome our cheers. Many citizens waved handkerchiefs or pieces of white cloth, symbolizing our acceptance of the new regime and our embrace of peace. It was amazing to see so many people cheering to welcome the Khmer Rouge. It was quite a scene. Some Khmer Rouge marched with brash or surly looks, their faces severe, while others appeared on edge, but this didn't trouble me much. I was just happy that, at last, the horrific shelling had stopped.

Our three-story house was one of five buildings comprising a complex that sat on Street 1074 near the main cross street of Mao Tse Tung Boulevard. Each floor was bisected by a long hall broken in the middle by a staircase, a total of six separate apartments. The first floor was reserved for father's grocery business. My parents occupied the second floor front. I had my own apartment at the rear. My grandparents lived in the front of the third story, and my sister Sy and her family near the stairs at the rear. Though Sy's marriage to Savoeun had been arranged, the two seemed a perfect match. Savoeun, in his thirties, was considerably older than Sy (in her teens), but he was very helpful at home. Even though he worked at the Interior Ministry, he always found time to lend a hand to our father. They'd recently presented the family with an infant girl. Their animated boy--four-year-old Vimol, who seldom cried or created a disturbance--often tickled the family with his bright, grown-up observations and was as polite as his father.

Our whole household--my sisters and I, parents and grandparents, brother-in-law, niece and nephew--was as happy as we could be. We'd endured four years of war, and so many of our countrymen had died. We were so happy that we kept our places with neighbors on our street and smiled at each other as we waited for the next group of Khmer Rouge to

---

[5] About 80 per cent of Cambodians are descended from people of the Khmer civilization, which flourished from the 8th to the 15th century.

appear so we could cheer them on too. Here, on our street, only small groups of four or five soldiers at a time marched by.

Finally, the war was over.

* * *

That morning, after all the cheering and waving, and thinking we were all safe, I decided to return to the hospital. I yearned to get back to the work I loved, and also, I had to retrieve my moped. It was less than two miles from my home to the hospital. I starting walking east on Kampuchea Krom Boulevard toward Phsar Thmei, the Central Market with its myriad of stalls and art deco design. Kampuchea Krom became a commercial area once you approached the Central market, and so the shops and restaurants were closed that day. The street was emptier once I got close to Phsar Thmei, except for group after group of Khmer Rouge either walking or on passing trucks. Not many people were on the street. As I walked through the city I began to notice things weren't as peaceful as the march of the small groups of soldiers I'd seen earlier in front of my home. Only yesterday, so many of us in my neighborhood had lined the street and cheered in welcome. Smiles were everywhere. But today, I saw none of this. At first I thought the Khmer Rouge might have heightened security in order to prevent looting. But before I reached the hospital, I witnessed a troubling scene. A group of several Khmer Rouge soldiers were shooting open the doors of a grocery store. They were making off with food and wine--especially wine, loading boxes of it onto two trucks. This struck me as odd since I'd heard the Khmer Rouge were very disciplined. I pretended to pay no attention to them and kept on walking. Some Khmer Rouge soldiers had commandeered mopeds and cars and, not knowing how to drive, crashed them into trees. Phnom Penh was like a new, alien world to these people from the countryside. Fighters on mopeds smiled broadly as they drove round and round in circles. It was chaotic, but the streets were otherwise largely empty.

At Monivong Boulevard, I turned south, and by the time I reached the hospital on Trasak Paem Street, *nothing* was right. I saw family members wheeling loved ones with IV lines still attached to their arms out to the sidewalk. Patients without family to attend to them were wheeled out by soldiers and just left on the street. Patients were being ordered out of the hospital without explanation. The first thought that sprang to mind was "Where is the mercy?" I knew the Khmer Rouge had battled the government and killed soldiers and civilians. They'd even planted bombs in cinemas, but I reasoned that it was because they wanted to overthrow the government and win the war. But they *had* won. The war was over now.

More than 90 percent of Cambodians are Buddhists. We practice *metta* which means compassion or kindness. To practice Buddhism is to offer help when we see someone hurting. Patients with an IV line clearly need help and yet were wheeled out to the street. What was happening before my eyes was not Buddhist practice. I'd heard General Lon Nol refer to the Khmer Rouge as "Tmil" which means "having no religion," but that reference meant little to me because up to that time I'd never seen a Khmer Rouge cadre. What I was seeing made me afraid to go to the hospital ward so I walked straight to my moped and rode home. By this time the Khmer Rouge had closed many streets. I had to find a different route to return home. I could see masses of people moving out of the city, but I didn't know why. Once I'd ridden farther than the central market area, there weren't as many closed streets. On our Street 1074, I saw only a small number of Khmer Rouge on foot. I thought most of them were probably concentrated in the city center. At home, I quickly parked my moped next to the stairway as usual and rushed into my father's shop.

I hurriedly told my parents what I'd seen. The radio was simply broadcasting over and over again news of the Khmer Rouge victory and playing Khmer Rouge songs. We listened, but there was no other special government announcement other than the condemnation of the "seven traitors" which included Lon Nol and Sirik Matak, the Deputy Prime Minister. By this time, word had already reached our neighborhood that we might all have to leave our homes. Other neighborhoods nearer the city had already been evacuated. We weren't sure if the evacuation affected the whole capital or only parts of it. Mother didn't want the family to be separated and asked me to get her sister's family to join us. Aunt Sok Kim lived only about three miles away, but by that time, the streets leading to her home were already closed. I had to return home without them. Mother was quite sad at not having everyone together, but nonetheless, we busied ourselves, preparing for the worst.

My father did most of the work of loading needed supplies and belongings into our Datsun sedan. Food and drink were paramount.

Clothes were bulkier and would take up too much room in the car. Meanwhile, my mother hurriedly searched for ways to hide the family's money and jewelry. She didn't want to secrete everything in one place so she sewed extra hidden pockets into some of our clothes. The rest of us stuffed some of our clothes and belongings into personal bags or backpacks.

As a medical student, I liked to always feel prepared--not necessarily for war, but for a family emergency, like an illness. My work in the military hospital had made me very conscientious about this. In my favorite red karate bag I had hydrocortisone to reverse allergic drug reactions. These were from a military base and so convenient to use. Powdered medication filled the top compartment of a vial and, with a quick push of the plastic cap, was mixed with a solution and ready for injection. I also carried several other intramuscular medicines. (Cambodian people prefer injections, even for the administration of vitamins or antibiotics.) In addition to these, I had antibiotic pills, various analgesics, and cough syrup. I also carried my stethoscope, some anesthetics, a scalpel, and sutures. And my medical school ID. I carefully locked my moped in the hope I'd be back in the near future. Though I love family pictures, I didn't take any albums with me for fear they'd be ruined. This could have been the best decision I ever made; it turned out that not bringing those pictures along may have saved my life. Any picture that depicted me as a medical student would most likely have meant my death. Once preparations were completed, we just waited to see what would happen next.

That night two soldiers came to our home. "For your safety, you must leave," one said. The new government was asking that all city people evacuate temporarily. "The Americans are going to bomb the city," he warned. Like everyone else, our family was being ordered to leave. Though the soldiers were armed, there was no obvious threat. Personally, I didn't believe the Americans would bomb Phnom Penh, but I couldn't see any other reason the Khmer Rouge would evacuate the entire capital. Everyone just followed the order without resisting. I think perhaps the word "temporary" was convincing enough to be accepted.

* * *

April is the hottest month of the year in Cambodia. It also happens to hold our New Year's celebration week with April 13, 14, and 15 the biggest days of the year. Everyone goes to the temple. At night, every street corner bustles with people playing cultural games, especially *"Chol Choong"* (throwing the Khmer scarfball) and Bos *Angkunh*. But that year, because of the worsening war situation, there were no celebrations.

Despite the oppressive heat, I had a *krama* wrapped around my head. I'd never done this before. Normally, we city dwellers didn't wear a *krama* to school or work. This multi-purpose rectangle of cloth symbolized peasantry, those who lived and worked in the countryside. It might be used by street vendors to cushion the head while holding merchandise. At home, we used it as a bath towel. Parents of a newborn might stretch it out to serve as a baby's hammock as my sister, Sy, did for her infant girl. But today I decided to wear it in the traditional fashion. It made me look like I was a peasant from the countryside--except that my skin wasn't dark enough. I actually liked wearing this checkered scarf because it's part of the Khmer-style dress, a Khmer symbol. I was a 24-year-old with no idea of what lay ahead, but this simple headpiece helped cement me to my homeland and who I knew myself to be.

Our family joined thousands of people evacuating the capital. With hordes of people completely filling the road, driving our car was out of the question. We also wanted to save gas, so we pushed it along the road.

A friend of mine covered his car with a Red Cross flag, thinking the Khmer Rouge wouldn't harm him or his family. Apparently, he hadn't seen patients being forced out of the hospital. I'd even seen bodies abandoned by families at the side of the road. During the evacuation, the price of food soared. People were still using currency then; no one could imagine that money itself would one day be useless.

As we moved slowly with the tide of human bodies, we saw elders abandoned at the side of the road--they were too old or weak to continue. Lost children joined these elders as the young and the old were culled from the masses.

The sea of bodies--men, women, and children--marched slowly along the pavement. Mothers with toddlers in hand moved slowly. Some people lofted umbrellas against the sun. Others pushed bicycles loaded with personal belongings. People had loaded two-wheeled carts with sacks of rice, baskets, and straw mats and hitched them to motorcycles. Some people hefted shoulder poles with loaded panniers and some carried baskets filled with vegetables atop their heads. In the distance, we could still see columns of smoke rising into the hazy sky.

Now and again, captured government tanks and trucks driven by the Khmer Rouge rolled noisily by. Some moved against the flood of walking people but wouldn't stop. People had to scurry to the sides of the road to avoid being run over.

At one point, I left the highway to fetch water from a well. Just before I reached it, someone saw me approaching and called out, "There're bodies in there!" Corpses had been dumped into the well by the Khmer Rouge to poison the water and sabotage the government by creating a water shortage. From that time on, at least as long as our reserves from home lasted, I used bottled sparkling soda--even to wash my face.

We went into hiding at my uncle's second house on the outskirts of the city in a somewhat remote village about six miles from our home. We'd only visited there a couple times. Uncle Chin Huot's two-story house was off Highway 4, a main road that led to Pochentong, the national airport and beyond. From time to time, Uncle Huot went there to relax. Uncle Huot was the most educated elder in the family as well as the wealthiest. (He proudly drove his American car, a Mustang, and liked to brag about it: "There is no stick shift, OK?") Chin Huot's government department job had him overseeing all the tax payments of the city's movie theatres, so many of the owners gave him special free movie cards which he then passed on to us. Besides the Cinelux French films that Nay Heng had favored, I loved the Chinese romance theatre, and with the free movie cards I could go to that theatre any day I wanted.

Because Uncle Chin Huot had a job in the Department of Finance, he "knew politics." We all had to listen to him because he was supposedly the smartest member of our family. He strongly believed the evacuation was only temporary, and, because we would all return to Phnom Penh eventually, his idea was to stay as close to the city as possible. "They're only evacuating people living in the city," he said. Here, we were no longer in the city. Besides, Uncle Huot said that once we were allowed to return, our home would be within easy reach. His house was well equipped to support all of us. There were several rooms to sleep in, the caretaker raised plenty of chickens, and there was ample water in the large cement water jars.

We had been forced to exit our own home via Highway 4, which led straight to the airport, but the Khmer Rouge hadn't been able to establish enough checkpoints to control the direction of the evacuation. So, once we got out of the city, we just turned off the highway onto the dirt road to our uncle's house. There were quite a few extended family members seeking refuge at the house, and with the caretaker's family, that meant nearly thirty in all.

Uncle Huot's caretaker was named *Ta* Kong (Grandfather Kong, respectfully, since he was only in his mid-thirties). *Ta* Kong was a pure Cambodian, dark-skinned with a large paunch, yet compact and sturdy from living a life on the land.

He raised chickens and essentially lived there to take care of the house. *Ta* Kong, his wife, and two children lived underneath. The name "Kong" means "safe" or "invulnerable"--a fitting name for a man who cared for us in this time of need. On the night of our arrival, *Ta* Kong showed us how to cook chicken rice. With so many mouths to feed, he first had to kill several chickens. Then he grilled them inside a metal container. When finished, he collected the chicken juices at the bottom to mix with the rice. It was delicious. We ate as if we were at a campfire with no thought of what was to happen next. We thought we were safe from any further forced evacuation. *This isn't such a bad place to hide out*, I thought.

But it seemed the Khmer Rouge goal was to evacuate *everyone*, not just those within the city limits. They'd begun with the city and then pushed outwards. The houses in this area were widely scattered, but one by one, residents were told to leave. It was only a matter of time before we, too, would be caught. In fact, the very next day a soldier in black came by and ordered us to leave. He made no threat and we didn't resist.

Even when we were all forced to leave his home, Uncle Huot stuck to his conviction: We should try to stay as close to the capital as possible. We listened to him and decided to go to a town called Kampong Kantuot because it was near Phnom Penh. And, very importantly, it was the village *Ta* Kong came from. *Ta* Kong suggested we go there, and Uncle Huot trusted him as he'd been the house caretaker for many years. Uncle Huot believed *Ta* Kong would do all in his power to protect all of us. We needed to travel farther south to be near water, and Kampong Kantuot was situated closer to the river. Naturally, he would accompany us. Everyone agreed. This, too, seemed like a good idea to me.

We ended up walking the 12 miles to Kampong Kantuot after the family car was "*sneu.*" The car was taken from us in the middle of the road shortly after we left Uncle Huot's house. It was the first time I'd heard the term used in this way. In the old days, *sneu* meant to "to ask for." But when the Khmer Rouge said it to us, it meant, *We're taking your car, and there's nothing you can do about it.*

* * *

At first, life in *Ta* Kong's village wasn't so bad. Kampong Kantuot was an old village and largely untouched by the war. We were given abandoned huts to stay in--one hut for all of us and, beside it, another for the Huot family. *Ta* Kong didn't live with us. He was classified differently: he was born here, he was poor, he was a farmer, and, as such, he was allowed to mingle with the Khmer Rouge villagers who were in the majority here. Not too many evacuees, city people, took refuge here. The only reason we were allowed to stay here was because *Ta* Kong requested permission from the Khmer Rouge. The hut we occupied was about head high so we had to bend down to enter. The roof was steep enough that part of it formed the two side walls. We had no beds. We slept on the ground. And with no bathroom, we walked out to the fields to relieve ourselves. This wasn't something particularly alien to us; after all, we told ourselves, this was village life, not the city. Each Khmer Rouge family, though, lived in a private hut. These huts were two-story pole houses, so they had a bamboo or wood floor to sleep on.

Perhaps because we were newcomers, the Khmer Rouge tasked us with light work. The Khmer Rouge chief would tell us what to do and where to go. This was immediately after the evacuation, and I suppose the Khmer Rouge work structure hadn't been well established yet. We cleaned up the grounds, gathered up downed branches, and hoed here and there. My grandmother was asked to chase birds out of the rice field. Every morning when I came out of the hut, there she was, sitting on a stool beside the rice field, waiting for the birds to land on the field. Then she would stand up, raise her arms into the air, and shout from the top of her lungs at the birds. Maybe because I'd never lived next to a rice field, I'd never seen anything like this.

Rice and food rationing hadn't yet begun, and we were able to subsist largely on the food stores we'd brought with us from home--mainly rice. In the capital, the Khmer Rouge demolished the National Bank of Cambodia. By this time, money was no longer useful. It had no value; the Khmer Rouge banned its use. My mother would trade articles of jewelry for rice and other food. I had no idea how she found persons to trade with, but everyone seemed to love gold, even the wives of Khmer Rouge cadre.

From time to time, the Khmer Rouge would assign some of us to assist with work in other villages, and because I was a young man, I was one of those selected to work outside the village.

The Khmer Rouge cadre that led my work group was an older man, in his late 60s or early 70s. He was tall and lean, and I admired him for his health as he strode barefoot and with purpose, his black pants down to just above his ankles. I actually had a hard time keeping pace with him. Every once in a while he looked back and flashed us a smile as if we were at once too young and too slow. He was very nice to us and very friendly. We walked all morning to get to the worksite, the digging of a canal. Beside it was a row of small huts. We were told this was where we would sleep at night. The floor of our hut was made of wood planks, and we were elated at the prospect of sleeping on a solid surface. I had nothing with me except a backpack that held an extra set of clothes, a light blanket, a metal plate, and a spoon.

Since we'd arrived late in the afternoon, no work was assigned to us that day. I'd never walked this fast for this long. My legs ached, and when night fell, I collapsed on the wood floor of the hut. With no electricity or even a candle, the night was coal black and stifling with the weight of the unknown as I set my backpack as a pillow and lay down shirtless on the bare floor. I looked up into black nothing and thought to myself: *This is my first time away from my family since we left home months ago.*

Even the night air was torrid. After a while, I began to itch, and so did the others. Before long I was bitten all over my body. I now realized the hut was infested with bedbugs. I knew what these bloodsucking insects were, but I'd never before experienced the maddening itching they cause. I couldn't see them, but I knew they were everywhere. About the size of apple seeds, they crawled out at night. None of us had any chance of sleeping that night. We went outside and slept on the ground instead.

We were tasked to help dig a canal, but after less than a week they sent me back to the Kampong Kantuot. The Khmer Rouge gave us food at work, but you had to carry your own plate and spoon. We marched off as a group with the Khmer Rouge cadre in front. At the time I had no thought of escape because the work was not particularly burdensome, and starvation had yet to appear. Anyway, where would I go?

It was in Kampong Kantuot that we lost Savoeun. One day, my sister's husband was taken away by the Khmer Rouge. This tall, spare man had won the family over with his gracious manner; he always bowed and smiled when he addressed someone. I was younger than he, yet he addressed me as if I was his older brother-in-law. "The organization needs him to help organize the new government in the capital," the Khmer Rouge cadre said. (Savoeun had previously worked in the Interior Ministry.) The Khmer Rouge led him away, and we never saw him again.

It was also in Kampong Kantuot that I first experienced what Cambodians call "*soch*." These extremely tiny bugs love to swarm over your head and bite your scalp. Usually, they appeared only in the early morning. Though they usually vanished before the heat of midday, these dreadful insects tormented us wherever we went. At first, I tried running away from them, but I soon learned this was futile. The only way to protect yourself was to wear a hat and wrap it tightly with the *krama*. (Sometimes, though, even this wouldn't protect you).

As much as I hated the *soch* and the bedbugs, there was something I hated even more: The Khmer Rouge in Kampong Kantuot began referring to us as the "Chinese family." Ever since I was a child, classmates had bullied and mocked me, accused me of not being Khmer. I am part Chinese and my given name is Chinese, but I never like being called Chinese because in my heart, I identified as being Khmer, as being Cambodian. In high school, we studied a poem by Krom Ngov that taught it was unwise to argue with the Chinese because they are smarter than the Khmer. Maybe this reflected the discrimination the Khmer practiced against Chinese people who carried on much of Cambodia's trade and commerce much as they did in other Southeast Asian nations. In any case, I was born in Cambodia and didn't speak Chinese, so I didn't want to be called "Chinese." It isn't that I was upset because I was born into a Chinese family, I was upset because of the way the Khmer Rouge addressed us.

They referred to us as Chinese--*the ones who didn't know how to farm*. They weren't merely referring to us, they were *mocking* us.

Because of this kind of discrimination--being labeled as Chinese, something less than Khmer--none of us were happy in Kampong Kantuot. After living here for about one to two months, my father suggested that we shouldn't stay in this village and instead, we should move on while we could, to Vietnam. This trip should lead us even nearer to water. That was my Dad's idea: get closer to a water source. When he was young, he'd transported palm sugar to Vietnam by canoe. He was a good swimmer and likely more experienced in getting food from a river.

My parents and grandparents were fluent in both Chinese and Vietnamese. At this point, we were actually free to travel in the sense that we could keep on walking until the road turned onto National Highway 2. That would lead us to Vietnam. My grandparents, however, wanted to stay in Kampong Kantuot because they valued my uncle's counsel, and since my mother didn't want to leave her parents, we all stayed with the single exception of the family of my uncle's in-laws, the Kimpau's family. They decided to keep on walking until they get even nearer to a water source. Their family of eight moved to an area near the border with Vietnam. Uncle Chin Huot's parents-in-law were with them.

And it was here, in Kampot Kantuot, that the Khmer Rouge began referring to us also as "new people," meaning people who had lived in the city. One day, after about four months in Kampot Kantuot, *Angkar*, or "the organization" as the Khmer Rouge cadre were also known, told us that the *new people* would be relocated to another area. The idea of relocating didn't alarm us. To the contrary, we were inwardly cheered by the news because we'd come to dislike this place. We weren't treated as fellow Khmer, one of their own. Tarred as "Chinese," we knew we weren't welcome here. Even though we'd be transported into unknown countryside, there was no sadness in our hearts and no tears were shed. We viewed this relocation as simply an extension of the new government's plan to temporarily evacuate people from the city.

Anyway, I thought, *could someplace else be any worse?*

Chapter 3

As our family plodded along the narrow, dusty road, the Khmer Rouge cadre told us we'd need to build our own shelters.

The air was dank, and by the look of the orange sun hanging in the hazy sky, it was late afternoon. I looked around. There was no village here. No houses. No residents. And, except for the dusty road we shuffled along, no evidence villagers had ever occupied this place. It looked like there hadn't been much rain lately. Because it was easier and everyone had something to carry, we walked in the middle of the road, between the deep oxcart ruts. Father, Chin Hor, and I carried the heaviest loads of rice and water; we divided the other reserves among my four sisters, my two young aunts, and my grandparents.

My sister, Sy, held her infant daughter. Her four-year-old, Vimol, was passed from one of my sisters to the other as my mother feared the curious boy would wander off and get lost. Mother kept stressing how imperative it was we all stay together and wanted me to make sure of it. Uncle Chin Huot kept his family together; each one of them also carried something.

By the time the Khmer Rouge told us we'd arrived, night had already fallen. Time was not on our side. We were among the first group to arrive here of thirteen truckloads of people. Each family chose its own location; many preferred areas under large trees and on higher ground near the dirt road. There was no electricity. No running water. No bathrooms. By the time our family was settled, it was already dark, and since we weren't at all familiar with the area, shelter-building would have to wait until daybreak. We slept on the ground. Some of us had hammocks which came in very handy. By now, we all knew that a hammock was a necessity.

I was a medical student, a city person (therefore a *new person*), and even though I was born in the countryside, I'd left it at the age of six. I had no idea how to build *anything*. Faced with having to construct a shelter, I felt next to useless. Thankfully, my father and grandfather were here, and they were very familiar with this kind of work. The next morning, with simple kitchen knives in hand, my father and my grandfather made straight for the nearby forest with me in tow. We walked deeper into the forest to gather branches and cut lengths of bamboo suitable to build a hut. At first, I just watched as my father and grandfather set to work cutting small and large tree branches. We gathered them up and carried them back to the site we'd chosen. The only real work we had at this time was building the hut, and we started to work right away to get the shelter up. My mother and sisters steadily tied the lengths of bamboo and branches, and, before long, we had a small hut for our family. We piled tree leaves on the top to make a roof, but when I stood inside and looked up, I could still see the sky.

I was surprised that somehow all the evacuees were able to build their own huts. Of course, some huts were stronger or larger or taller than others depending on the builders' ability. People who had tools completed their huts faster. Those who didn't waited until they could borrow tools from others. Over the next few days, more new people arrived, and the area got crowded quickly.

We'd brought enough rice and food with us to last for a while, but we knew our reserves wouldn't last for long. My mother and sisters crafted elongated cloth bags to hold rice. This way we could tie the ends of the bag together and hook it over our shoulders. It made carrying rice much easier. Somehow, my mother came up with the thread, needles, and material to do all of this. Her resourcefulness played a big role in our resettlement.

This place seemed quiet and safe. To relieve yourself, you peed a few yards behind your hut. I was also getting used to squatting. We used paper from books and newspapers for toilet tissue. Before long, though, human waste was everywhere. With masses of people crowding the area, we had to be careful where we stepped.

We'd barely had time to settle ourselves before the Khmer Rouge forced us to move again--this time, deeper into the jungle. We were ordered to leave our huts in order to make room for more incoming *new people*. The order came without warning and Khmer Rouge cadre stood by ready, then and there, to guide us to a new location. At first, I had no idea what had happened or why we had to move again. We just did what we were asked to do. I caught on later and had reason to believe the Khmer Rouge intent was to deprive us of all precious or valuable belongings. Their philosophy was to rid us of everything we had, including jewelry and rice, prized possessions each of us tried hard to hide. I believe the Khmer Rouge knew the majority of us would hide valuables by burying them so, with surprise orders to leave, the majority of us would have no chance to unearth our possessions.

· We were finally settled in a desolate area that offered nothing but empty field after empty field. It was barren even of trees except for a few tamarind, *krasaing*, and kapok. And even these weren't abundant. But I began to see a few scattered structures here and there on the road that indicated people had lived here in the old days. A few structures were quite large and off the ground, very similar to what we call "*sala chhan*," a structure found in Buddhist temples and reserved for people to gather and eat during festivals. To issue instructions, the Khmer Rouge gathered us together on selected large areas of higher ground next to the pond. The pond was only half full and covered completely with water hyacinth except directly beside an old wooden walkway. A few large trees stood on this higher ground. I imagined it must have been very peaceful here in the past.

But there was no time for us to enjoy nature. We didn't know what would happen next. It was here that I saw more "old people" (people who had joined the revolution earlier). Rows of small houses in the village belonged to the *old people*. The *old people* here had been given direction from *Angkar* to prepare to welcome the *new people*, us. Judging by their huts, they had been here many months before us. They had buffalos, cows, and oxcarts as well as a large structure that served as the commune dining area, the "cuisine."

* * *

The Khmer Rouge divided the country into regions. Our region was in the province of Pursat located southeast of Battambang. Anything north of Highway 5, next to Tonle Sap, was designated "*Dambon 4*" (region 4). Our region was called "*Dambon 2*," the part that was on the south side of Highway 5. This village was called "*Mok Chhneang*." *Chhneang* is a woven bamboo basket similar to a two-handled basket, but without handles. Fishermen use a *chhneang* to dip into shallow water to catch fish. The word "*mok*" means face. Some people called this village "*Moat Chhneang*," meaning "the mouth of the *chhneang*." Others called it "*Khmoach Chhneang*" which means "Ghost *Chhneang*," this to stress the potential tragedy we all faced. Thousands of *new people* would eventually be sent here.[6]

By now, our family realized that we were captives in a prison without walls. We were surrounded by empty dirt fields with few fruit trees. And, except for the hyacinth-covered small pond, there was no water nearby. We weren't allowed to build a hut beside those of the *old people*. The Khmer Rouge assigned us to a plot of land on the lower ground, and we built three huts--one for my family of ten: my parents, my five sisters (Sy, Suor, Ky, Lay, and Sam Ang), my niece, Vimol, and me; one for my grandparent's family of five: my grandparents, Chin Hor, Leang and Dy; and one for the Chin Huot family: Chin Huot, his wife, and their four children.

The village of Mok Chheang was about a four-hour walk from Highway 5. Four hours from the highway didn't seem far, but *Angkar's* rule was very strict: we were not allowed to leave the village without permission. The Khmer Rouge reminded us at every meeting: "Do not dare to block the revolutionary wheel." In other words, we were obliged to follow *Angkar, the organization*. And here, we saw Khmer Rouge women carrying rifles. By now, we'd left everything behind us, including our illusions.

The Khmer Rouge village chief in Mok Chhneang was known by his nickname, *Ta* Kdam, literally "Grandpa Crab." Grandpa Crab was in his forties, and maybe he'd been given this name because of his homely appearance. Short and stocky, he was often shirtless. A life of constant physical labor had sculpted muscled arms, but his fingers splayed out like crab legs, and his satchel mouth showed protruding front teeth that were uneven and stained black. His skin was dark, the mark of all pure Cambodian farmers. I hardly ever saw him wear long pants, only tattered shorts that exposed strong, muscular calves developed by chasing after buffalos across farmland both wet or dry. He was always barefoot. From his manner of speaking I could tell he had no formal schooling. I knew he didn't read or write Khmer. He had an assistant, *Mit* Sam (*mit* for "friend" or "comrade"). *Mit* Sam was a former law student who'd married

---

[6] Counting four other nearby villages, the number of persons settled here would reach 30,000.

27

the daughter of *Ta* Kdam's relative; no doubt this was the reason he'd been selected.

* * *

Being a medical student, I thought I'd prepared well to care for my family. I had my stethoscope, blood pressure cuff, syringes, medications, injections, and pills. Cambodians held a belief that the more serious the illness, the more imperatively a person needed an injection. A few years before the Khmer Rouge took over the country, my father had expanded his business to include part ownership of a pharmaceutical store, and as a medical student, I got into the habit of collecting various medicines. I created my own emergency kit. It included band-aids, bandages, sutured instruments, sutures, emergency IV medications, analgesics, antibiotics, and so on. When someone in my family got sick, they could count on me. I started by watching a nurse who used to come to our home to care for my grandfather; he always had an emergency kit filled with all kinds of medications.

My work in a military hospital gave me access to an American surgical kit that came in a soft, khaki folding case. Inside there was a strap to secure each instrument in place. I loved this kit because even though it was compact it had all the instruments I might need in an emergency, and I loved American products. For instance, the medication came in a powder with a mixing solution built-in. With a simple push of my thumb I could instantly produce a solution for injection. I loved to collect these types of kits and medicines. They often came in handy, and I left Phnom Penh with my emergency kit and a bag full of medicines. Each time we moved, my father was able to hide the lot. I used the medicines to trade for rice. Mother used her jewelry to trade, but this lasted only about a year.

* * *

It only took about six months for things to fall apart.

Initially, our assigned job was to prepare the rice fields for planting. This area had been abandoned during the course of the war so the dirt hadn't been turned over for many years. There weren't enough buffalos or cows to plow the ground. Each of us, a *new person*, was given a hoe and ordered to walk in single file to the fields. When we reached the work area, we were told to form a line at the edge of the field. The majority of us had never even held a hoe in our hands, let alone used one. In spite of being soaked by early rains, the ground was still hard to dig through. We set to work. Every time the hoe hit the ground I could feel the pain in my hands. Within a couple of hours, I started to see blisters on my palms. (Later I learned to avoid blisters by keeping a tight grip on to the handle.) By the end of the day, everyone was exhausted. In our previous lives, before the revolution, we'd worked in shops or businesses or gone to school. Now, every day, from morning until sundown, our job was to break up hardened soil. Toiling in the fields made me appreciate the lives of farmers.

Angkar had not given us enough food so we had to supplement the meager rations with what remained of our own food reserves. My uncle, Chin Hor, having also been my classmate in medical school, had a very hard time adjusting to field work. He was depressed and was criticized by his mother--my grandmother--for not bringing anything with him from the city the way I had. Grandmother desperately wanted to be able to trade possessions for rice as I and my parents did.

Starvation stalked us like a jungle beast. When food became desperately scarce, my sister Sy did the best she could to feed and take care of her baby. The infant (whose name has been lost to me) was small and born only a few months before the Khmer Rouge took power. The baby cried all the time because she was always hungry. My sister was unable to nurse. As she became starved, her breasts dried out, and her baby was the first to die in my family. When the baby died I was sad, but at the same time, relieved because I knew she wouldn't have survived. No matter what we would have tried, the baby would have died anyway.

With the burden of endless field work, Chin Hor's mood darkened. If the person working beside him accidentally splashed mud or water in his face, his temper flared. Before long, Chin Hor developed a large ulcer on his foot. Work became impossible. The Khmer Rouge denied him rations, and he lost weight fast. Chin Hor was the first person I ever saw waste away. He lost weight faster than any of us except for my niece, the infant. This early starvation, coupled with his depression, meant his death early in the revolution.

It was hard to believe that only a few months out we now had two deaths in the family. Conversation among family members wilted; most of the time, we no longer talked. Exhausted and hungry, each of us retreated into our thoughts. How could life have turned out this way?

* * *

The Khmer people were being killed by torture, but they were also being worked to death. They died from forced labor, illness, and starvation. The change from a healthy, well-developed body into an emaciated one is too fast for anyone not to notice. At first, the victim loses weight. Then the body swells. Finally, the person becomes emaciated. Death follows. With the enhancement of the cheekbones and the intrusion of the temporals, people begin to resemble living skeletons and become unable to express their emotions by facial expression. It's like watching leprosy eat your body away, and yet feeling powerless to do anything but pray for the starvation to end.

I began to wonder if we were living in what the elderly people had called "the land of the pregnant men." *Could the ancient Buddhist prediction be true?*

Before I experienced starvation, I never thought a human life had seasons. But going hungry taught me there are two seasons to a human life: a *starving season* and a *not-so-starving season*. The *not-so-starving season* lasted only a couple of months at harvest time, usually November and December. The other ten months of the year was the *starving season*.

My grandfather taught me that to avoid bad karma I should never kill living things. In the old days, he used to buy cages of birds and set them free so as to liberate "*toukha*," sorrow, misery, or suffering. Once, I asked my grandfather who, prior to the Khmer Rouge takeover, had been a faithful Buddhist, "How could all Cambodians suffer the same fate at the same time? How was it possible that millions of people did something bad in their past lives and were now receiving karma at the same time?" He had no answer. Living in the killing fields, seeing suffering, death, and dying every day, I came once again to believe in fate and luck. After all I'd seen, I came to believe faith wouldn't deliver me from death.

Later, when starvation conditions worsened, I saw my grandfather sitting beside a small dirt hole, fishing for frogs.

* * *

The Khmer Rouge divided us into groups based on age and sex. Elders were to remain in the village to tend gardens. Their job as gardeners was to plant foods like potatoes, pumpkins, cucumbers, and so on. Older women were tasked to gather cow manure and were also charged with the care of small children. One woman was ordered to breastfeed children even though she knew she was unable to nurse.

The elders were also tasked to make rope needed to tether cows or buffalos. Rope was made from palm tree branches. There were too few palm trees in our area so the branches were brought in from elsewhere. The elders pounded each branch with a wooden hammer until it became soft and fibrous. Then the fibers got teased into small strings that were reinforced and finally woven into longer and stronger ropes. I'd never seen this before. The benefits of the palm tree surpass any tree on earth. The palm is so useful to Cambodians; we eat the fruit buried inside its hard shell, and the leaves can be formed into mats or hats or even the roof of a house!

Elders were also responsible for producing nails. The Khmer Rouge didn't believe in religion even though *Angkar* knew that 90% of Cambodians practice Buddhism. *Angkar* believed that Buddhism emphasized "not working" and therefore contradicted their revolution which demanded communal labor. They believed that a monk's only activity was to stand in front of people's houses to "beg" for food so they denounced monks, calling them "parasites." Under the Khmer Rouge, all Buddhist monks either disrobed themselves or were forced to abandon the saffron. The practice of Buddhism, a bedrock of Khmer society, was forbidden. Temples, formerly sacred places, were turned into pillage grounds. The Khmer Rouge ordered us to destroy every structure in the temples, including the stupa (funeral monument) to retrieve the steel rods used to reinforce the cement. The rebar was brought into the village for the elders to heat, mold, and cut into nails.

The Khmer Rouge allowed married couples to stay in the village, but they had to work in the rice fields nearby. So I lied to the Khmer Rouge. I told them that I and my sister Sy were husband and wife, and that Vimol was our son. Vimol was a very smart 4-year-old. He called me "*Pa*," meaning "dad," because I told him to do so. He was a clever child; I told him once, and only once, and he always remembered to call me "dad."

The younger children were to pick up cow manure used to fertilize the rice fields, and the teenagers were grouped with peers from other villages to form what the Khmer Rouge referred to as the "front force"--which really meant digging canals.

My younger sisters, Suor, Lay, Ky and Sam Ang, were in the teen group, and so they were forced to leave the village to work in different places. There was no way to communicate with family members. I heard from them once in a great while when their labor group passed through on its way to other places. We never knew where they were going or when they might pass through or return to the village.

Once, one of my sisters, Suor, tried to come home for a brief visit. Suor's personality and drive would have carried her far in a world of formal education. She was a thoroughly modern girl; she dressed in bell-bottomed trousers and wore bright colored blouses. Bespectacled and very outgoing, she presented herself to the world as so up-to-date I often thought my parents wouldn't be able to arrange a marriage for her when the time arrived. As independent a girl as Suor was, it wasn't surprising that she should take it upon herself to defy *Angkar* to visit us. She was caught by the Khmer Rouge, and, as punishment, they tied her up for one day in the sun. When I heard this, I went to see her. My sister was swollen from head to toe from severe malnutrition. Meeting her in this situation was meaningless in that there was nothing I could do to help her. We looked at each other, asked each other about other members of our family, and prayed for each other. That's all we could do. Later, I heard from one of her friends that she died. That was 1975, Christmas time. That's how I remember it.

* * *

In the Khmer culture, no matter how old you are, if you still live with your parents, you usually don't make important decisions on your own, even when it comes to finding a spouse. Though I was a 24-year-old, I'd hardly made an important decision without consulting my parents, particularly my father. As a matter of fact, besides choosing medicine as my career, up to this point, I'd never made any significant decision on my own.

Here, in what would come to be known as "the Killing Fields," I was young, relatively healthy, and one of the strongest of all the members of my family and, in the sense of formal schooling, probably the most educated. Taking stock of myself, I decided it was time for me to be in charge. I wanted to show my parents that I could help the family. Even though mother had already traded most of her jewelry for rice, I still had plenty of medications left, so I went out trading myself. Medication was practically nonexistent so pills had become valuable. I could even trade them a few at a time. A bottle of 100 vitamins would last me a few months. We all knew that a few vitamins wouldn't do anything to benefit a starving person, but when it came to their parents or children, people clung to the hope that it might help.

By now, the famine was real. Of an original population of 30,000 persons, only 3000 remained, most having perished. By the end of 1976, five villages were combined into one. *Angkar* directed us to move out of Mok Chheang to another village, Svay Chhrum, whose name means "lots of mangos."

But there were no mango trees here.

* * *

You might think education wasn't important in that era, because educated or not, your job was ordered by the Khmer Rouge. We weren't allowed to choose our jobs; we all labored. But I looked at things differently. No matter where you were, no matter what situation you faced, having a better education could give you an edge for survival. It allowed you to come up with ideas that might help you. (The Khmer Rouge didn't know how educated I was; otherwise, I would not have been spared).

My father had always stressed the value of education. "An educated person is a person with a brain," he liked to say. He always reminded me that your brain is the one thing no one can steal from you. And, in trying to survive the *starving season*, my brain told me that the job I should seek was the one that would give me access to food. In other words, a job as near to the kitchen as possible. In those days, my friends and I called the kitchen the "finance department." The Finance Department deals with money, and if you have money you can buy food. Here we no longer used money, and so the kitchen was the only place you could find food "legally." I began by just hanging around the kitchen, what the Khmer Rouge called "cuisine" (French for "kitchen"). This seemed strange, considering the majority of the Khmer Rouge came from remote areas and were illiterate and uneducated, but whatever they called it, I called it the "finance department."

Since we'd arrived here, our family had forgotten what sugar tasted like. I had managed to save one bottle of cough syrup, the only bottle I had for my whole family. So, finally, one night I decided to mix the whole bottle of cough syrup into our large pot of rice porridge. That night, we all savored the taste of sugar. We looked at each other and smiled. That simple rice porridge seemed as if it was a fine delicacy served up at a fancy restaurant.

We came to measure time by our stomachs. We were allowed one hour's rest for lunch, but it took us less than a minute to eat it. It took longer to retrieve the ten-person bowl from the kitchen and to distribute the gruel equally among each group of ten persons. Ten ladles for ten people. One ladle per person. That was it. Once it was on a person's plate, he could consume it in just one slurp, which many did. But some of us just took time to "enjoy" the taste of rice. We called it *Preah Meh*," which means "God's rice." Others took this time to look for extra food. As starvation gripped more and more people, they began searching for anything edible--insects, crabs, plants. Other desperately hungry people were driven to stealing cucumbers or pumpkins from the communal farm, but not me. I was always afraid of being killed by the Khmer Rouge, and fear was greater than hunger. Instead, I devised a plan to hang around the "cuisine" as much as I could. Only the *old people*, the Khmer Rouge, were allowed to work in the kitchen. As a *new person*, I was new to the *organization* and, therefore, not to be trusted. Without being asked, I began helping out in the kitchen. I washed pots and pans that were left outside. The *old people* who worked in the kitchen came to love me because I did this outside of my regular work in the rice fields.

When field work finished at 5 pm, we all returned to the kitchen for dinner. After dinner, I hung around the kitchen to help. Sometimes, if I were really lucky, I could collect some fish scales that were left outside after the cook prepared fish. I would dry the scales and eat them as extra food. Before I washed the pans, I collected every single grain of rice that was stuck to the inside and ate them as fast as I could in order to avoid being caught. Most of the time these leftovers tasted sour because they were old, but it was still better than not having anything to eat. I thought back to the conversations of the elders so long ago as we were trucked through the deserted cityscape of the capital concerning the old Buddhist prediction: *"There will be houses where no one lives; there will be streets where no one walks; and people will be so starved that we will eat a grain of rice that stuck to the dog's tail."*

* * *

Every time I saw the kitchen run short of water, I grabbed two buckets and went out to fetch it. I worked slowly, day by day, to gain the trust of the *old people* until, finally, I was chosen to be the water fetcher for the kitchen; in fact, that's what they called me: the "water carrier." As a *new person*, I still wasn't allowed to actually work in the kitchen, but I was getting closer to my goal. Two large cement jars sat outside the kitchen, and my job was to keep these cement jars full at all times. Every morning, I carried two water buckets to the canal and fetched water back to the kitchen. This meant I had to make as many as 20 to 30 trips to the canal every day. Still, this job wasn't as grueling as digging canals or preparing the rice fields, or even as difficult as minding and feeding the buffalo.

Sometimes the Khmer Rouge asked me to gather the small children into a line. These were children who were too young to be sent out to work; that is, younger than five. The children's feeding time was before the adults'. The children had to form two lines facing each other with their plates set on the ground in front of them. The food rations were distributed by the "foundation youth," the *komar moulthann*. The "foundation youth" were the teen or pre-teen children of the *old people*. To the assembled children, it must have seemed like I was working with the Khmer Rouge, but to the communists, I was just another *new person*, doing what he was told while trying to survive.

Each *new person's* child was given a ladleful of watery rice with salt. If they happened to be lucky that day, each of them would receive a few drops of soy sauce. One of these children was my nephew, my "son," Vimol.

One day, just before the *komar moulthann* giving out soy sauce reached Vimol's place in the line, the teen ran out of soy sauce. I watched Vimol as tears first welled in his eyes and then ran down his cheeks. He'd *so* looked forward to those precious few drops of sauce. My heart was torn because I couldn't do anything about it. I couldn't show favoritism to my *son*. In any case, I didn't have access to the soy sauce.

One day, sometime after this, the Khmer Rouge asked me to help the kitchen in the field far removed from the village. I decided to take Vimol with me because I knew that if he were with me in the field he would have a greater chance to eat. Out in the field there were plenty of foods for Vimol. Those days, when we talked about food we literally meant "watery rice" because at mealtime there was usually nothing else but that. However, this was the harvest season, and the rice was actually *rice*, not watery gruel, and there was soup and even meat to go with it.

On his first day in the field, Vimol saw a fish on his plate, not just soy sauce. He was so happy that a smile spread across his face. "I have fish!" he even bragged aloud. I couldn't help but enjoy this moment and the feeling that *I'd* made this decision, and it had turned out to be the right one.

* * *

Within two days, Vimol became sick.

I had no choice but to carry him back to the village. I was so upset with him. I'd planned and carefully worked my way into the best job possible, working with food service in the field. Now, if we had to return to Svay Chhrum, *both* of us would miss out on the food available here.

Vimol started vomiting. His condition deteriorated rapidly. In less than a day, he was too weak to walk. He'd become dehydrated from the constant diarrhea of dysentery. Vimol remembered seeing me give injections to others in the village. He looked at me as a medical doctor, and at first, he begged me to give him a shot to make him better so I wouldn't need to take him back to the village early. I was so touched by his request. Such a bright and mature mind at so young an age! But by this time I'd run out of all medicines. I told him I didn't have a shot to make him better. We had no other choice. I lifted him onto my back, he put his arms around my neck, and we started back that morning. It was such a long walk it took us all morning to reach the village. Walking across rice fields wasn't that easy carrying Vimol on my back. His chin pressed into my shoulder with every step. Each rice field is bounded by a raised dike of dirt to contain water and to allow people to walk outside of the actual field. The dike was about two feet wide and very slippery at the beginning of harvest season due to the rain. Slippers were useless; most of us went barefoot and by then, I'd gotten used to it. Still, trying to balance on the slippery rice dike was a bit difficult. But once past the rice fields, the land turned level and dry.

I'd crossed so many fields that by the time we reached the road, I was very tired. Vimol's chin pressed onto my shoulder the whole time. At first, the pressure of his chin on my shoulder hadn't bothered me much, but as time went on and I walked farther and farther, his chin began to feel heavier and heavier on my shoulder. Eventually I couldn't handle the discomfort. "Lift your head," I told him. "It hurts." Several times I told him to keep his chin off my shoulder because it caused me pain, but he didn't seem to listen. After what seemed a long time, I couldn't stand it any longer. I jerked him off my shoulder so I could look him in the eye and scold him face to face. Immediately, I saw he was so weak that he couldn't control his neck.

I couldn't believe my eyes. Only a few minutes before, he hadn't been this weak. He'd lost control of his neck muscles.

"I'm sorry," he managed to say in a small, weak voice. He was so dehydrated he had no tears. Of course, I realized then that Vimol had tried to respond to my repeated requests but just lacked the strength to do so. As he talked, his head hung down. He could no longer look up into my face, his *dad's* face, a face that *could* still cry, a face with tears streaming down.

I picked him up carefully so as not to hurt him any further and walked the rest of the way to the village. I made no more complaints of my shoulder. By the time we reached our hut, Vimol was even weaker. With a voice so faint that I could hardly hear him, he asked me for fish. He was hungry. I don't remember exactly how, but somehow I managed to find a small fish for him. He grasped that fish in his fist and then died before he could eat it. I sat there for I don't know how long staring at his lifeless body, the fish still in his hand. I had no idea what to do next.

By this time, I'd witnessed so many deaths, but nothing touched me as deeply as the death of Vimol, my *son*. It had been my decision to take him out to the field kitchen--me, the educated one, the fourth-year medical student. And I've always wondered, if I hadn't taken him out to the field, would he have survived the *starving season*?

And I also wonder: Where was God? God is supposed to be able to see and hear *everything*.

Couldn't He see Vimol?

Couldn't He hear that whisper of a voice asking for a fish?

Chapter 4

With Vimol's recent passing, my sister, Sy, had lost not only her husband, but both of her children. Only four of our family--my parents, Sy, and myself--remained in the village now. My grandparents had died before the real famine began. My younger sisters, Lay, Ky and Sam Ang, were out in the front fields. We had no news of them. Starvation continued to stalk us. Vimol's death had devastated me, but our struggle to survive the *starving season* went on.

The majority of us *new people* were now either living alone or with the few surviving family members. With ongoing famine, the real meaning of the Khmer Rouge doctrine *"Sak norna kbal nak noeung"* now became clear. Speaker after speaker harangued us: "If it is your hair, it must be your head" meaning you alone are responsible for your actions. If you steal and are caught, you alone are responsible. However, I grasped the actual meaning: *You are on your own. No one else will help you.* This dogma changed Khmer society significantly. It forced each of us to think only of ourselves. If I shared food with others, there might not be enough for me and so I might starve to death. It was increasingly difficult to live in a society that placed oneself above others. Yet--we were starving. Snakes, earthworms, raw fermented fish (*prahok*) crawling with worms--starvation forced me to eat these things. I thought back to one day when we were living with *Ta* Kong. He'd gathered of bunch of palm fruit. With his dirty knife he cut the top shell off the fruit. Then he scraped the fruit from the side of the shell with his thumb and offered it to me. I saw the nail of his right thumb was black and coated with dirt. "I don't like palm fruit," I lied. Now I was in a fight for survival. I ate just about anything--dirty or not.

Life had become simple, but hard. Simple because there were only three things to do every day: work, eat, and sleep. According to the Khmer Rouge, there wasn't even a need to think. "Let *the organization* do all the thinking," we were told. But that's the hardest part about being a human being--not thinking. The Khmer Rouge told us this over and over. "All you have to do is to follow *Angkar*; don't place your hands or legs across our historic wheel; the wheel will break anything in front of it."

Saturdays and Sundays ceased to exist. We received a work break every ten days. But this "work break" didn't mean free time. It was during the "break" that we were forced to attend commune meetings. First, we were lined up in rows, and then we sat down on the bare ground to listen to *Angkar*.

The Khmer Rouge directed us to call one another "comrade, not "Mr." or "Mrs.," because these words implied that the person addressed had a higher status than the speaker. Under the revolution we were supposedly all equal, and therefore, "friend" was the "proper" way to address each other.

We were also no longer permitted to use the word *"chumreap suor"* which means "hello" because in Cambodia if you say this in greeting to someone older than yourself, you must also *sampeah*, placing both hands together in a prayerful gesture of respect. The Khmer Rouge claimed this demonstrated the different levels of Khmer society. The Khmer Rouge preached that we were all at the same level: no one was superior to another. Therefore, to *sampeah* each other was no longer allowed. Shaking hands was also abandoned because it was said to derive from a "foreign" culture.

At every meeting the message was the same. The speaker began, "I respect and salute every father, mother, and comrade."

Then the speaker would continue:

> *You are gathered here today to listen to our organization. Our organization is a revolutionary organization. It was born from the immense sacrifice of our people and our soldiers in the front fields. The level of revolutionary consciousness of our people is very high, and this is how we can eliminate all of our enemies. You are safe now because of our marvelous soldiers and organization. In order to respond to this monumental sacrifice of our brothers, our organization is asking you to focus on your work as strongly as you can--the way our soldiers are protecting us from enemies like the imperialists of America. We started our revolution with our bare hands just like we now use bare hands, but with the guidance of our organization, our country will advance by leaps and bounds*

to become the strongest country in the world. No one will dare to challenge our revolutionary soldiers. Today, other countries are in awe of our revolution. Other countries are amazed by our revolution and the organization that can build the very largest dams and dikes and canals using only our hands and hoes. It won't be long until our country will be so productive that we will have machines to feed us. We won't need to feed ourselves. The machines will feed us. So do not do anything to hinder our revolution. Do not put your hands or legs across the revolutionary wheel. If you place your arm in the wheel, your arm will be cut off. If you place your leg in the wheel, your leg will be cut off. Our organization will scatter any enemy that dares to challenge our revolution. The enemy can never hide from us. Angkar has more eyes than the pineapple. You are either for our evolution or against our revolution. We are determined to destroy the prior imperialist culture you were exposed to and replace it with our revolutionary culture born from our peasants. We no longer have any prisons. We simply eliminate our enemy. To keep an enemy is no gain, and to be rid of an enemy is no loss. We are determined to enforce our revolutionary guidance and path.

When you first arrived here, our soldiers deprived themselves in order to offer you the rice and other foods you are eating now. This is the sacrifice our combatants made for you. Do not forget that you came here with nothing.

We no longer have exploiters or the exploited. We will live happily from the result of our labor. You do not have to be afraid to leave your doors open. There are no thieves, no criminals, no prostitution. The only society we have is equal, peaceful, and prosperous. And, above all, there is no unemployment. Everyone has work to do. It does not matter if you are children, youths, middle-aged, or old. We all have work to do--work that was assigned by the bright, revolutionary spirit of Angkar.

Fathers and mothers--abandon your past. You should stop thinking about the past. You lived in an imperialist society. For the good of the people we must totally wipe out and completely destroy that society, the society that was full of evils, full of the enemies of the people.

Stop hugging or embracing the old society. Start welcoming and accepting our new society, the greatest, brightest, most prosperous, most glorious, and flourishing society. Leave the thinking to our organization. You must imitate our combatants. They have given everything to Angkar including their blood and flesh. Leave your children to Angkar. They will be watched by our most devoted, conscientious people with a very high revolutionary awareness. All you have to do is to follow the guidance of our organization. Nothing is simpler than this.

Every speech was delivered in lengthy, repetitive monotone. Every speech was identical to the one before it, just recited by different chiefs. First the village chief gave the speech. This was then followed by a speech by military personnel. The military speakers always had an M-16 on their shoulder. They wore either green or black uniforms and wore Chinese PLA caps. These military people were usually from the "regional" headquarters. They never walked, but instead rode black bicycles with attached radios. They turned on these radios when they rode, and revolutionary music signaled their approach.

The purpose of these speeches was to strengthen our belief in *Angkar's* "great stride forward." They repeated this again and again, at every meeting, from one chief or soldier to the next. The vocabulary they used was very similar to that of the broadcasts from Peking. (When I lived in Phnom Penh I sometimes listened to Peking radio.) The Khmer Rouge, like the Chinese, always inflated their messages with adjectives like "great," "immense," "marvelous," "miraculous," "supreme," "grand," "luminous," and so on.

None of us really listened to these speeches. We just pretended to listen. At the end of the speech, or whenever we were told to do so, we shouted "Chey Yo! Chey Yo!" ("Victory! Victory!") We were told to raise our right arm three times as we shouted. Before the revolution, I'd never seen gesturing like this. In the past, if we agreed with a speech, we just clapped. (And we did it without being reminded.) But now, agree or not, I shouted and pumped my fist into the air along with everybody else.[7]

This speech-making, however boring, did provide us one valuable opportunity though: the chance to search for head lice. The person seated behind me crushed the lice on my head, and I did the same for the person sitting in front of me. When we found lice we popped them between our thumbnails, and the stink rushed into our noses. After the pop you would feel a tiny liquid that rushed out of the lice and stained your nails dark. Except for not eating the lice, we weren't much different from monkeys. After a while, this foul odor became part of our lives.

Unless you shaved your head, you had lice. Everyone had lice. In previous times, girls or young women wore their hair long. It wasn't uncommon to see a girl with hair below her waist. After the revolution, however, the Khmer Rouge preached that growing long hair meant a person was trying to cling to "old imperialist dogma." Long hair, they told us, was for the old, imperialist society, not for our "revolutionary" working

---

[7] Besides efforts to influence us through repetitive, boring speeches, the Khmer Rouge broadcast songs over loudspeakers installed on high poles or trees. The "music" used traditional melodies and instruments. A song for revolutionary soldiers reminded me of my own life: "When walking, walking barefoot/Crossing mountains for months over rocks and stones and thick forest/Sleeping on the ground with a torn plastic sheet/Sitting and shivering in the pouring rain/Later, getting to sleep in a hammock/Taking the silent forest for a temporary home/Sunlight cannot get through, in the dark with mosquitos/Feverish from malaria, shivering but determined to be brave/Only one pair of trousers and a shirt for the body/Rotten and torn/With every washing, sitting and waiting and shivering/Once dried, rewearing it and going back to work in the village." The Khmer Rouge national anthem, however, repulsed me as it repeatedly referred to "blood."

class. So, all women had to cut their hair. At first, this was hard for some, but at least they had fewer head lice.

* * *

When I first left Phnom Penh after the evacuation, I refused to eat rats. My parents had made sure we brought plenty of food reserves with us when we were forced from our home. But that was *before* the famine. I was introduced to rats when I was in Kampong Kantout, the first village we went to. There I was told that people ate rats in the old days, but these were rats that subsisted on rice from the fields. I'd lived most of my life in the city, and so my only knowledge of rats was that they lived around filthy habitats and fed on trash. And I *hated* rats. But not anymore. Now, in the *starving season*, I considered it the luckiest of days if I had a rat to eat.

In order to survive, I learned how to build rat traps. Rats live in holes they create on higher ground. A square of wood with dirt on top was propped up by a stick. Every morning a young boy named A Touch set up the traps on any dirt mounds he could find. A Touch was an expert at choosing the trap locations. A young teen, and fast, he laid anywhere from five to ten traps a day, and, if we got lucky, we trapped one or two. One day we caught a pregnant rat with many embryos in its stomach. It was our lucky day!

At first, the only way I could eat a rat was roasted because the meat was dry and crispy, but as time passed--boiled or roasted--I no longer cared. When boiled, I got to drink the soup. Eventually though, we had to give up roasting rats because the smell would alert the Khmer Rouge, and their rules became stricter as time went on. *Angkar* did not condone the private practice of cooking outside the commune kitchen. So--boiling it was.

There was never enough water. We were allowed to shower every few weeks depending on *Angkar's* "vision." We never brushed our teeth. There weren't any toothbrushes. I was taught by friends how to use dirt to brush my teeth. You pinched pieces of loose dirt between your thumb and index finger and then rubbed it on your teeth. Then you simply gargled with water--if there was any. But, about the only time you had access to water was when you were at the kitchen, and that was infrequently. If you worked in the rice fields, you used muddy, yellow water to rinse your mouth. There were no toilets. No toilet tissue. No soap. When we squatted we used leaves or twigs. If there were none, then we used pieces of dirt or a rock. Dirt clods. I never thought that could be possible, but that was the way we lived. And there was no water to wash our hands afterwards, either.

* * *

By now, I was getting closer and closer to the four *old people* who worked in the kitchen, and I could tell that they'd begun to trust me a bit more. Every day, I grabbed two kitchen buckets and walked a couple dozen times to the canal in order to keep the cement water jars filled. The buckets were suspended from a yoke made of bamboo. The best yoke had a bit of flex. I had to walk in rhythm to avoid spilling water, but it didn't take me long to master this.

I worked at gaining their trust until, eventually, they allowed me to spend the night next to the kitchen as a few of them did. I tied my hammock to the support posts of the dining area. Here, every night I told the "Foundation Children" made-up stories so I could even be closer to them. I remembered Chinese fiction I'd read in my junior high school years. Between those tales and the Chinese movies I loved, I could easily make up stories for them. After all, these children represented another source of food. From time to time, these children of the Khmer Rouge would sneak food to me. Sleeping next to the kitchen, I was always by myself so it was easy for them to sneak food out to me. The food wasn't from the commune kitchen but from the huts of the *old people*. This was my nighttime food. Even though my job as "water carrier" gave me occasional access to kitchen vegetables like cucumbers, potatoes, or pumpkins, I didn't dare steal from the kitchen. I couldn't risk losing this job. Or being killed. However, I did occasionally receive extra food from the kitchen staff and so was able to bring some home to my parents.

* * *

One day, the second chief of the Khmer Rouge in Svay Chhrum, *Ta* Nget, began screaming at the top of his lungs, "Water carrier! Water carrier! Water carrier! Where are you?" He was running through the village and shouting as he looked for me. I could hear him at a great distance. The whole village could. Even in ordinary times, he was known for his booming voice.

I ran out to him as fast as my legs could carry me. As soon as I saw his face, I knew there was trouble. His voice was steely.

"You just gave an injection to one of our soldiers and now he's in trouble."

By then I'd become close to *Ta* Nget. He knew that I was "an intellectual," yet in spite of his indignant manner this day, he usually treated me well. He even knew that I was a friend of *Mit* Sam.

A Khmer Rouge soldier had come to visit his family, and the *old people* in the village needed someone to give him an injection. The soldier already had a vial of Streptomycin with him. All I had to do was to inject him. So I had. Now, I rushed in to find this soldier suffering a severe allergic reaction. I dashed back to my hut, grabbed my last remaining vial of Hydrocortisone, and sprinted back to the soldier. I thumbed the soft cap of the bottle to mix the medicine and injected him immediately. His rash soon disappeared, and before long he felt better. In the excitement of the moment, my training and skill had taken over, and I felt no fear of acting. Later, however, I realized that on that day, my life had hung by a thin thread, indeed.

Thanks to an American vial of hydrocortisone, my life wasn't over yet.

* * *

From time to time, I was sent to catch fish for the kitchen. This was one of the best parts of my job. The canal wasn't too far from the village--just a couple of hours' walk. By now, this didn't seem far. In the morning, I dug for earthworms for bait. In the late afternoon, I would walk to the canal and lay out my fishing lines. Then I would sleep on the ground overnight beside the canal. Sometimes, I surprised myself with my own proficiency: Never in a million years did I think my life would be this way. Before this, I'd never fished. My grandparents had taught me never to kill living things--even bugs. This is a basic proscription of Buddhism, but now I'd learned how to find the best spots to dig for earthworms, and I wasn't afraid to cut them into pieces and slip them onto fishhooks. And now I knew how to set up a fishing line. The fish line was long, and I stayed in the water until all my hooks were baited. In the morning, I would go back into the water, pull out my lines, and collect the fish for the kitchen. At first, it was no simple chore to unhook the fish. Their fins and sharp spines easily cut my hands, but after countless pricks, I learned to grasp the fish tightly. The best thing was to not be afraid and just hang on tightly. The water was only thigh-high, and I was alone. I was given rice to bring along and could eat whatever fish I wanted. At sunset, and again at sunrise, I reveled at the sight of palm trees standing out against the sky in serene beauty. Everyone wanted this job. Who wouldn't?

Every time I emerged from the water, though, my legs were completely covered with bloodsucking leeches. When I plucked them off, blood ran down my legs, but this didn't bother me a bit. Maybe I had no fear because this was the last thing I had to worry about. Many people did fear them, though. I remembered my sister Suor telling me that the thing she feared most was leeches. In order to get to the rice field, she had to cross the canal, the one that was infested with them. In those days, women didn't wear regular underwear, and what they feared the most was that these worms could get into their privates.

One day, the kitchen staff asked me to slit a rooster's throat. Of course, I'd never done this before and felt very uneasy about it. But I had no choice. Once I managed to get a hold on the rooster, I bent its neck backward and made the cut--but I didn't make a clean one. When I set the cock down, it took off running. I bolted after the hapless bird, chasing it around the dining area while everyone laughed at me. By the time I got to it, the rooster had already died. It turned out the experience of killing a rooster wasn't as bad as I thought it would be because it generated a lot of laughter.

But the one act of killing I just couldn't perform was to dispatch a monkey. Once, one of the kitchen staff tied a captured monkey to a post. I was supposed to kill it with a club. The line, however, was long enough that the monkey could run in a circle. As soon as the monkey saw me approaching with the club, the poor creature raised its arms. It was no different from seeing a human being attempting to protect himself from being hit. When I managed to miss striking a blow, another person took the club from me, and, with a single blow to the head, the monkey was dead. I could kill worms, rats, snakes, fish, or crabs without hesitation, but when it came to a monkey, I just couldn't do it.

* * *

I remained vigilant. I was always looking for ways to feed my father and mother and my sister, Sy. One day the Khmer Rouge was organizing a sizable group of people to transport rice and palm sugar from another village--at least fifteen oxcarts, with other villages sending their own teams as well. It was a two-day trip to the warehouse. I saw this as a great chance to help my father, and I begged the chief to allow him to join this group. I knew that any time you made a trip out of town like this, chances were, you would be fed better--that is, at least better than those confined to the labor camp. Though I was fed better than others because of my work for the kitchen, I still wasn't able to sneak out enough food for my parents and Sy. So, to have my father out of the village to fetch rice and sugar with the labor group would be the best opportunity for him to be fed better. My father was so pleased when he heard he'd been selected. I warned him that those sacks of rice he was supposed to carry were quite heavy. Each rice sack weighed at least fifty kilos, but he said he would do anything for this opportunity. I knew my father. Even before the war he was a very hard working person. When he was young, he used to carry heavy loads of palm sugar to Vietnam. Every morning farmers climbed the palm trees and placed elongated bamboo containers underneath the shaved palm flowers. The next morning they collected the containers that more often than not were filled with palm juice. From this juice, palm sugar was made. I thought father was still strong enough to carry heavy rice sacks in spite of his age.

Days later, when father returned to our hut, he told me he'd hurt his back while carrying a rice sack. As he talked to us, I realized his body just wasn't as strong as I'd thought. As aged and starved as he was, he had to lift those heavy rice sacks. In fact, he told me everything had gone well until one of the sacks he was hefting had gotten caught on the edge of a roof and pulled him backward. He immediately felt his back snap. From then on, father was no longer able to work. The Khmer Rouge stopped his meager food ration, and his condition worsened.

Those who couldn't work were often sent to the *frightening place*, the "hospital." Everyone feared going to the hospital because once you entered it, death was almost unavoidable. The hospital was the place where the living traded places with the dead. Unable to do anything, father lay on the floor of the hut he'd once helped build. Yet, he refused to go to the hospital.

Chapter 5

"Father is dead."

My sister woke me up in the middle of the night. I was sleeping in the dining area next to the commune's kitchen, not too far from our hut.

Sy led me through the darkness to our hut. As soon as I entered our hut I saw my father's body covered by his faded blue blanket.

"He either fell from his hammock or fell down when he went outside to urinate," my mother said. "I heard a noise. I came out, and he was already breathless."

I had no tears in my eyes. I took it as another death in the family. What else could I do? We had all expected this to happen. Under the Khmer Rouge regime, father wasn't working so he was not qualified for food. He wouldn't go to the hospital. He had turned into a skeleton before our eyes.

I felt little sadness at father's death.

This way, his spirit could rest in peace.

That's what I told myself.

I asked my friend, *Mit* Cheum, to help me bury my father. *Angkar* didn't allow us to travel at night so we had to wait until the morning to prepare father for burial. We wrapped father in his blanket. Then we tied both ends of his hammock to a long bamboo pole and used his hammock to carry him. Mother reminded me to be sure to bring the hammock back so we could replace it for a torn one in the future. Hammocks were very essential to everyday life those days. Mother had made hammocks for all of us early on when we could still afford it.

Mit Cheum and I dug a shallow grave not too far from the village and covered him with loose dirt. That was it. Only *Mit* Cheum and I were there. Sy and mother were too weak from starvation to leave the hut.

My niece, grandparents, Uncle Chin Hor, and my *son*, Vimol, died before my father, but I could no longer remember how they were buried, or who had buried them. *I just don't remember.* This was the first time I could remember burying someone. The sad thing was this person happened to be my father.

Before the war, when someone in the family died, all the other family members and guests gathered to mourn the death. Then we would all form a funeral procession and walk to the gravesite. The deceased would either be cremated or buried in a chosen place. Before the war, it had been our family's practice to attend to my great-grandparents burial place. At least once each year, we brought food, fruits, and fake money to the tomb. First, we helped each other tidy the area, ridding it of grass and leaves, spider webs, and dust. When we'd finished cleaning up the area, my parents would set fire to the fake money to symbolize the transfer of wealth to our ancestors.

But on the day I buried my father, there was no procession of family or guests. There were no family members in sight. Only *Mit* Choeum. Under the Khmer Rouge, family sentiment was forbidden. There was no ceremony. No mourning. Only a deathly quiet and lonesomeness. The Khmer Rouge reminded each of us to think about *Angkar* and country first, not the family.

I was very saddened by how my dad was buried--even more saddened by this than the fact that he was dead. Giving him the chance to join the work group outside the village had cost him his life. And now, after his death, I couldn't even bury him in a decent manner. I thought of doing something to mark his grave, but then I realized even this wouldn't do any good. Without Khmer Rouge permission, I wouldn't be allowed to come back out here. Neither would I be given the time to visit his grave. With the starvation we were facing I might not even have another chance to return. Life at that time was always unpredictable, and I knew it wouldn't be long before father's gravesite would be a rice field.

My thoughts took me back to a time when I couldn't reach the fruit of the kapok tree. Father was still strong those days. I had no idea how to pick the fruit. But he knew how. He grabbed a stick about a half-meter long and threw it high into the tree. Sure enough, a few fruits fell. With a few more throws, more fruits fell. We gathered them up, smashed open the fruit, and burned the cotton out of the seeds. Then we ate the burned seeds. The seeds were hard to chew, but they were our food. The black seeds turned even blacker when they were covered with ash. We picked the seeds out one by one and tried to blow the dust or ash off, then ate them to ease our hunger. Our lips were blackened by the seeds. The seeds looked like pepper seeds and when we chewed them, their black fragments stuck between our teeth and gums and made us look like old men with badly decayed teeth. Our hands were also stained black, but that didn't last long with the kind of labor we were doing. Whenever we could find the chance, we would sit under a kapok tree and enjoy our snacks--just the two of us, father and son. Father knocked down the fruit with his well-aimed throws, and I prepared the snacks. Those were good times we shared. Now he'd left me before I had a chance to return him some favors.

With his death, the thought plagued me that I had never done a single good thing for my father.

And there was another memory that forced its way into my mind. It was the time *Angkar* brought us soda from the city. It was the one and only time I tasted soda since the Khmer Rouge had taken over the country. Even then, the Khmer Rouge bragged about the "generosity" of "our comrades" from the city. "Our comrades do not forget us here," they said, "and we will remember them by sharing our rice with them." On that occasion, the cadre brought crates of orange soda into our village. I was tasked to line people up in single file. My father joined the long line with everyone else. I was told to pour some soda into each person's cup. Once a person had received his ration of soda, he was to return to work. One by one, I poured orange soda into each person's cup as they passed, occasionally looking into their faces. From time to time, I glimpsed a smile. I saw gratitude, too, on some faces. *The gratitude of an injured animal.* I poured carefully. And poured again. A careful pour, person by person. I had to carefully ration each pour. Each person was so pleased to receive this rare favor. I was almost beginning to enjoy this assignment. I poured and I poured. Eventually, I found myself looking into the face of my father--for a second time. He had rejoined the line.

I stood there on the torrid hardpan, frozen, the soda bottle in my hand. I stared at him. I didn't speak, but my eyes said, "Father, you mustn't do this."

He, too, stood unmoving. He faced me with an expression that begged for another taste of soda. And as he stood there facing me, the cup empty in his hand, I could clearly see something else in his eyes--the unmistakable look of disappointment with his son.

Perhaps the Khmer Rouge wouldn't catch us, but any person in line might report us. I dared not take the chance. I was afraid to lose my job. I also feared a simple act of favoritism would cost both of us our lives.

* * *

Every time I think of my father, I ask myself why I was so afraid of doing this good thing for him, why I was so selfish. From the day I entered medical school, father showed nothing but a wholehearted commitment to help me. Once, he came looking for me at the hospital. When he spotted me, I was wearing my white coat, and a stethoscope dangled from my neck. He didn't say anything, but I saw him staring at me in awe. I was the only one of his children to advance beyond high school. From the look on his face, I knew he was so proud of me. But then, later, back at that soda line, I was not sure what he thought of me. I cannot forgive myself, and now I have to live with this burden, a weight much heavier than any rice sack my father toted, a weight I cannot put down.

* * *

I was distraught over the fate of my family. Why did God allow people in my family to suffer, people who never done anything wrong to anyone? Right after we'd first been evacuated from Phnom Penh, a friend of my father's, the owner of a pawnshop, had offered him a bowl of watches, a full *bowl* of watches, at least fifty of them, in return for a debt he owed my father, but my father refused them. He said that at a time like this, we shouldn't think of anything except trying to survive with what we had. Afterwards, from time to time, father would refer to this "mistake." But then, he would add, "We might as well stop thinking about it. It wasn't meant to be." Our lives would have been different if we had all those timepieces. We had no way of knowing that watches would soon become one of the most sought-after objects. The Khmer Rouge loved watches. You could trade watches for more rice than anything else except gold.

Strange. I don't think the Khmer Rouge even knew how to tell time.

* * *

My parents and grandfather taught me that if we wanted to be safe and happy in life, we needed to follow the Buddha's Middle Way. But no matter how much good they did, they continued to suffer. My grandparents had died not long before the famine began. But they were old, and I couldn't--didn't--expect them to survive. But why my father? And Vimol? He was only a child. In his short life he'd never even had a chance to do anything wrong. And why did millions of others perish? Where was God's mercy?

God had no mercy on our family.

If I could speak with God, I would ask Him what else we had to do to get his blessing.

If following the Buddha's Middle Way didn't spare our family, and that spirit they called "God" was both deaf and blind, then who would help us? Who were we to depend on?

This is my father's ID photo that was discovered in my sac-a-dos during the search for a tobacco thief. Its possession could have cost me my life. The only picture I managed to bring with me out of the killing fields, it now commands a place of honor in our home.

My mother's picture was given to me by my mother-in-law after the war.

My five sisters. (From left to right: Sam Ang, Ky, Lay, Suor, and Sy. Lay and Ky were separated from us early. I never heard from them after they left to labor in the "front fields."

My sister Suor was a thoroughly modern girl. Bespectacled and very outgoing, she presented herself to the world as so up-to-date I often thought my parents wouldn't be able to arrange a marriage for her when the time arrived. As independent as Suor was, it didn't surprise me that she would defy the Khmer Rouge to visit us.

My sister, Suor, and my mother's sister, A Dy, at Uncle Chin Huot's second home during before the war. After we were forced into hiding at this house, "Grandfather" Kong cooked rice and chicken for us.

Me, as teenager

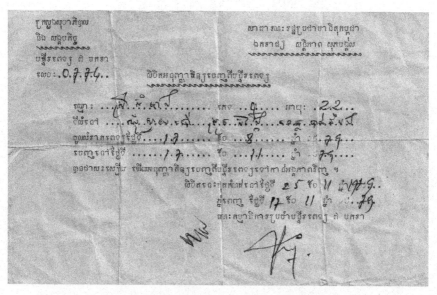

On Sunday November 18, 1979, the day we'd chosen to leave
for the border, all of the medical staff was scheduled to visit Tuol
Sleng, the high school that the Khmer Rouge had transformed into
a torture center. I forged a patient discharge letter for use by Srey
stating that she was released from the January 7th Hospital and was
to return home to Svay Po in the western province of Battambang.

On the letter, I used my sister's name, "Sam Ang," instead of
Srey's. I signed it with the letter "K" representing my friend's name,
Khoy You Deth, who had left Phnom Penh a few weeks earlier.

Dr. Bill Heegaard had a twin brother, and before he left KID he gave me a gold coin, explaining that his twin had a matching coin. He stressed that it was a gold coin so if I needed to I could trade it for currency. He said he carried this coin to bring him luck and hoped it would bring me luck too. I never need to sell it.

Our shorter gold necklace with a pendent of the Buddha.

Our first pictures taken inside the KID camp after we received our tracing numbers identifying us as "legal" refugees. I couldn't have been any happier than this.

Srey and I and Chanthy Yi in our hut at Khao I Dang.

On my second day in the camp, I started walking from the camp entrance, passing ward after ward, paying close attention to the sign posted on each- German, French, Japanese, Thai Red Cross, Catholic and so on. Finally toward the end of the complex, I found this one. I walked inside and (in halting English) asked to be a volunteer.

Dr. Haing Ngor (at left in front row) with ARC staff. Later, he would win an Oscar for the role in the acclaimed film "The Killing Fields"

Dr. Daniel Susott who I work with on ARC Ward One has
changed our lives and the lives of our children. Without
him, Sakona, our first son, would not have been born an
American citizen ten days after we arrived in Honolulu.

กรรมการประสานงานองค์การช่วยเหลือผู้ลี้ภัยในประเทศไทย

2948 บี. ซอยสมประสงค์ 3 ถนนเพชรบุรี กรุงเทพมหานคร 4 โทรศัพท์ 252-5904 โทรเลขย่อ–REFUGEECOM

To whom it may concern (ICEM/JVA):

I have examined Cambodian Refugee Chum Rim Ly in Chon Buri Holding Center awaiting resettlement in the U.S.A.
Her pregnancy is not more advanced than 6 months (by examination and detailed questionning of dates – some confusion was cleared up).

To delay her resettlement would cause much avoidable suffering at this point, prolonging her stay in the dismal camp situation and requiring the baby to be born in sub-optimal conditions.

Committee For Co–Ordination Of Services To Displaced Persons In Thailand
2948-B. SOI SOMPRASONG 3, PETCHBURI ROAD, BANGKOK 4, THAILAND. TEL. 252-5904
CABLE ADDRESS: REFUGEECOM TELEX: TH 2779

This is one of Dr. Daniel Susott's letters. He stated that on July 27, 1980 he had examined my wife in Chonburi, and her pregnancy had not advanced more than six months.

I urge all persons concerned
to do everything within their power
to facilitate this family's
resettlement in America.
Chum Kim Ly's husband has
been accepted to finish medical
school in the U.S. and must
be there in August. "T" NUMBER AND
THEY HAVE THEIR
SPONSOR.

Thank you. Contact me
if I can be of
further assistance.

Daniel Susot MD
medical coordinator
CCSDPT

Chamnam and I watch chidren at play at Khao I Dang. If I hadn't encountered friends like Chamnam at the desperate, chaotic place that was Camp 007, Srey and I might have been trapped in a lonely and precarious life there. This fortuitous meeting changed my life. We remain in contact to this day.

On her way to retrieve water, Srey posed with a new
friend, Noy Stevaux, one of the American nurses who
volunteered to work on the American Refugee.

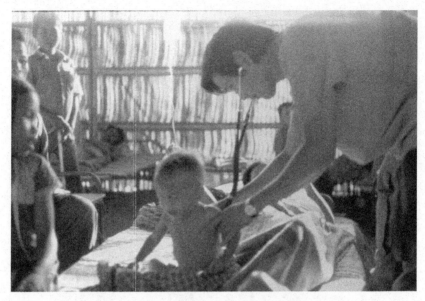

I examine a young patient on ARC Ward One. Karen
Johnson, another staff of ARC, gave this picture to me.

Dr. Khiev Sam, Dr. William Heegaard, and I at Khao
I Dang. Dr. Heegaard incised and drained a peritosillar
abcess troubling Dr. Sam. Dr. Heegaard gave me his lucky
gold coin at his departure from KID. I cherish it still.

The ARC team hosted a farewell party for us. After seven months in Khao I Dang, we were so happy to leave, knowing that we were taking another step closer to America

At the airport, Chris Feld, Debbie Tate, and Dr. Haing Ngor were among the friends who came to see us off. I whispered to myself, "I was chosen," a realization that overwhelmed me.

Dr. Daniel Susott snapped this photo of us just before we boarded the plane in Bangkok.

Sakona, our first son, was born ten days after our arrival
to Honolulu. My wife and I were so happy he was born an
American citizen that we named him "Free Bird."

A visit from Dr. Bo Sin, my wife's aunt.

"Free Bird," our first son, brought us boundless joy.
(Of course, I carry a packet of color prints in my pocket.)

Our three children today: Kosal in his Pulmonary Critical Care
fellowship at UC Davis. Sakona ("Free Bird") is an Emergency
Medicine Physician and currently serves as Medical Director
of the Emergency Department at Kaweah Delta Medical
Center in Visalia, California. Sakara is an internal Medicine
resident at Santa Clara Valley Medical in San Jose.

Chapter 6

Toward the end of 1976, starvation reached a peak.

Even rats were in short supply. Ninety percent of the city dwellers had died in less than two years--so many *new people* had died that the initial five villages were combined into one. I knew this because *Mit* Sam, the former law student who served as Grandpa Crab's secretary, had become a friend and shared that information with me.

The kitchen where I used to work was eliminated. As more and more people died, the number of kitchens was also reduced. So I lost my job.

With that loss I grew more desperate in my efforts to survive. One likely job was to labor in the rice fields, but I didn't want to work outside the village. Plowing fields would be very difficult for me; the mud was knee-deep in places and I knew I wouldn't even be able to pull my legs out of the mud, let alone chase the buffalos. I might as well not even try.

I said earlier that I wouldn't venture out to steal things because I feared getting caught. That's not entirely true. There was one occasion, as the beast of starvation clawed at me, that I risked all and followed others into the night. Once, with a couple of friends, I snuck out into the cucumber fields on a moonless night. It was so dark I couldn't see any cucumbers. I didn't want to kill any of the plants so I was careful not to disturb them. I sat down in the dirt and slowly swept my hands back and forth through the black. My friends couldn't believe what an incompetent thief I was. At their urging, I soon learned I wasn't going to find any cucumbers in the dark this way. I learned that all you have to do was to walk all over the field, "shoeing" all over the plants, and, when your foot touched a cucumber--voila!--you picked it. But no matter how hungry I was, I didn't return to the cucumber patch on subsequent nights. I feared being caught. And killed.

I'd lost my sister, Suor, the year before on Christmas Day, 1975.

My sisters, Lay and Ky, departed with the youth group, and I never heard from them again.

Sy suffered from a large wound on her right leg. In those days, we were almost always barefoot. If you developed a sore on your foot while working in the rice fields, the wound would never heal. Sy tried everything she could think of to help the wound heal. This included applying a traditional Khmer healing technique for sores on the leg--applying a rub of crushed, burned frog. But her wound wouldn't heal, and since she could no longer work, the Khmer Rouge cut off her daily food ration.

My mother was still surprisingly strong considering her age, though much of her energy was directed toward finding ways to help Sy.

My sister, Sam Ang, worked in the children's group and was still alive.

Uncle Huot and his family had moved from our village to another village beside Highway 5. After this, I never heard from him again, except on one occasion when I was assigned to pick up salt for the village at the train station. I saw Uncle Huot standing there. His face was swollen, as were his legs. I didn't expect him to survive.

Just when I wasn't sure what would happen next, I learned about a new position being created in the village. At one of the communal meetings, the Khmer Rouge announced they were looking for volunteers to join a new team--the "fertilizer production team."

"This is what revolution is all about," they said. "We have to forge our own destiny. We have to come up with new ideas to make our country prosperous. You do not have to ask *Angkar* for help. This is called 'the owner of actions or work.' We depend on no one but ourselves. If farming three times a year is better than once a year, and it is possible, we are determined to make this happen. Finding ways to make our farm more productive is our job. This is the only way to show *Angkar* your 'strong stance' in revolution. And today we need your help by converting our waste into fertilizer to improve the productivity of our rice crop."

Having announced this, *Angkar* directed the young children to collect bones from the corpses uncovered during field preparation. The Khmer Rouge had earlier directed children to pick up cow manure from the road to be used as fertilizer, but now they were also ordered to collect bones. They were then to pound or crush the bones into powder and throw it back into the fields as fertilizer.

The work of the "fertilizer production team" was considered to be a "difficult" and not an "honorable" job (as all other labor was called), and therefore team members would be given extra rice compared with other work rations in the village. It was to be a small team, only six or seven members. The assignment was to collect human feces from the toilet pits and dry it for use as fertilizer.

Doing this job would allow me to stay in the village with mother and Sy, and it didn't seem to be very physically demanding. What did I have to lose? The main problems I'd have to deal with were the smell and contamination, but I was willing to try it; I didn't want to starve to death.

In those days, a dozen portable toilets had been built in the village. Workers dug a large hole in the ground, placed two wood boards across the hole for people to squat on, and covered it with a portable shed. Each morning the fertilizer production team went from one shed to the other, lifting the shed and setting it to one side to uncover the pit.

To scoop the feces, we tied a piece of tree branch onto an American-made soldier's helmet (The Khmer Rouge called this a "Lon Nol head" because they considered Lon Nol less than feces. After he'd seized power in a military coup, he embraced pro-imperialist America and was blamed for allowing the U.S. to bomb Cambodia.)

We mixed the feces with rice husks and laid it out on the fields until it dried. Then we cut it into squares, collected them with our bare hands, and bagged them for use as fertilizer.

The stench was beyond words. At first, just the sight alone nauseated me: Small worms wriggled everywhere in the pit. You couldn't even see the feces because they were completely covered in worms.

Scooping the feces using a helmet tied to the end of a stick wasn't an easy task either. We had to come up with some material to tie the pole to the helmet. *Angkar* provided only the bare minimum in necessary materials. We were supposed to be "the owner of our work," and so had to come up with materials ourselves. The only string we could find was unsuitable. Sometimes it would come undone, leaving the helmet inside the pit. Then we had to retrieve it with our bare hands and reconnect it to the stick.

There was no water nearby. Toilets were built some distance from the commune to avoid the odor. Our hands were always dirty, and the only way to dry our hands was to use dirt or we just dried our hands on our clothes. Every time I thought about this work, I wondered how I could survive such insanity. On one hand, I wanted to scoop as much as I could each time. On the other hand, I couldn't hold my breath long enough for one scoop and ended up scooping quickly just so I could breathe again. It was vital that we work fast and collect as much as possible because *Angkar* always gave us "direction" for each job. Many bags of fertilizer had to be filled each day. The Khmer Rouge threatened that a lack of speed in accomplishing our task symbolized a "sabotage mentality."

After we collected the feces we mixed them with rice husks. This was the easy part of the job. The nose-piercing stink was diminished, we were in the open air away from the toilets, and the rice husks covered the feces so the wriggling worms were less visible. We spread the mixture to dry on the empty rice field in a thin, single layer. Under the summer sun the drying process didn't take long. By the time we were spreading the last of the pastes out, the early pastes had dried enough to be bagged. We then cut the layer into square pieces with a hoe and bagged them. Pieces of dry mixture broke loose constantly. We could use a hoe to try to collect these, but it would take forever so we just used our hands. I couldn't believe that I would do this kind of job, but I had no other choice. I set health and sanitation aside. I had become a slave to my own hunger. All I wanted to do was to live through this *starving season*.

Initially, the "fertilizer production team" was fed better, but after a short time, we were reduced to nearly the same meager, daily ration received by other laborers.

I grew even more desperate. In order to stay alive, I knew I needed to come up with another idea.

Finally I decided to forge a note transferring myself to the *frightening place*, the "hospital." The note I forged was brief. It stated that I was from the "field" meaning the rice field (the Khmer Rouge called the rice field the "second battlefield;" the first battlefield meant the military battlefield), and was being sent to the hospital because I was too sick to work. I knew I'd probably not be challenged. First, hardly any Khmer Rouge could read. Secondly, they didn't really care about "patients." *Angkar* believed that those who "liked to stay" in the hospital were lazy and didn't want to be part of the revolution. Such people end up dying anyway, they said. The Khmer Rouge repeatedly harangued us: "To keep you is no gain, and to waste you is no loss."

I needed to conserve as much energy as possible, even if it meant eating less than I already was. I was convinced this was the only way to stay alive. Instead of chasing buffalos and struggling in the mud that required a lot more energy, I preferred to stay on land. Even though scooping feces was such a job, I soon realized the energy I expended at this work was more than the calories I was receiving.

* * *

The "hospital," the largest structure I saw in those days, stood on a flat piece of hardpan and was nothing but an old cow barn. It had been built a long time ago, certainly before the war. It was to shelter cows and buffalos at night. It had no walls. In the old days, villagers would build a fire to produce smoke to prevent mosquitos from biting their animals. During the revolution, the Khmer Rouge turned this aged animal pen into a "hospital." Next to it they built a smaller structure for the "hospital directors" and the "nurses." A building beside it served as the kitchen.

No one had maintained the main structure, the cow barn. It was abandoned during the war, and the roof was full of holes. The sky was clearly visible overhead. It was an open structure; there was nothing under the roof except the support poles, which had once served as hitching posts for the animals. When it rained, all of us moved to the middle area to avoid being soaked by windblown rain.

There were never fewer than a hundred patients a day, all crammed into eight rows. The aisles served as walkways for the "doctors" to do their "rounds" and to distribute food. We lay on the ground next to each other in assigned rows. No mats or any kind of ground cover was provided. Each patient had to provide his own. If a patient didn't have one, he just lay on the bare ground. Each patient (if he was lucky) had his own small bag containing some clothes, usually a torn, dirty *krama*, a hammock, and spoon. That was all anybody had.

We had to seek out patches of ground beneath undamaged roof. We covered ourselves with the old, torn, and smelly blankets. The blankets were never washed. Not only because there was no water, we had no strength anyway. Why care about washing blankets? Most of the time the blanket wasn't even ours. It was just taken from someone who had just died. It was too heavy to carry around in our bag, and so whenever we found another

75

one, we just used it. All we cared about was getting enough food to keep our hunger at bay. The "hospital" was mostly silent. There was hardly any conversation among patients. We had nothing to talk about. Besides, we were too weak to talk. Everyone just sat motionless and held onto the blanket or else curled up on the dirt floor. In the rainy season, usually July through September, falling rain was the only sound. Otherwise, the barn was silent. We lay in rows on the ground like living corpses. We didn't even have strength to brush the flies from our faces. Shooing them with our hands was useless. The flies always came back. They settled on our lips and dug into either our eyes or the smelly, dirty blankets stained with food or urine. Some people completely covered themselves with their blankets, trying to avoid the flies, but when it became unbearably hot you had no choice but to uncover yourself--either that or risk suffocation.

Besides the silence, despite the presence of a hundred or more people, there was almost no movement. The patients were so weak they barely moved. Even looking closely, the only movement you could see were the flies that surrounded each patient and the barest movement of the patients' chests as they struggled to keep breathing. Their eyes were closed, their faces expressionless. From time to time, the slow motion of a hand shooing flies was visible. Life was lived in slow motion. Our bodies had become so emaciated, we had little strength. Whenever we had to rise from a seated or squatting position, we had to lift our buttocks first, then use our hands to push ourselves up from the ground before using our knees to straighten up. The whole world stood still. That was us. We stared blankly into space and waited for our time to come. There was nothing we could do to change it.

Now, I had become one of the starving. No one could help anyone. Everyday, at least a dozen of us died. The bodies were tossed onto an oxcart and dumped in the fields nearby.

Every day.

* * *

There at the hospital, one day I met my two aunts, A Dy and A Leang, two of my mother's twelve siblings. Though they were younger than me, they were my aunts. They used to look completely different, but starvation had made twins of them. Both were emaciated, their eye sockets sunken, their cheekbones protruding, and their cheeks caved-in. Twin skeletons.

Just skin covering bone. They'd been sent here from the fields because they were too weak to work. They hardly could walk. We smiled at each other. That was all.

I was sure starvation had done the same to me, but with no mirror, I couldn't see myself. A few days later A Dy and A Leang both perished, their bodies tossed onto the oxcart and hauled away. I didn't cry at all. I was actually glad to see them leaving a twentieth-century hell.

Every day a dozen bodies were removed, and another dozen came in. The "hospital" was simply a place to die. It was a place to trade the dead for the dying.

In the first few days I was in the hospital, seeing the people and the conditions they endured, I asked myself many times if I'd made the right decision in choosing to come here.

Seated on the ground beside my assigned space, an area no larger than a coffin, I leaned against a post and closed my eyes. My stomach cried for food. I let my mind wander. I thought of one of our fertilizer team members. During our work breaks, this young man liked to lie in his hammock and write down lists of ingredients for meals. A strange thing for a man to do. (In those days, cooking was "woman's work.") He was about my age and rather quiet. He never shared information about his life. He had no friends. After work, he always retreated to his hammock to be alone. Once, I asked him, "What's the point of writing a cookbook at a time when we can't even find rice?"

"You have to use your imagination," was his only answer.

One day, he didn't show up for work. We found him in his hammock, dead. We used the scraps of his cookbook to wrap dry leaves as cigarettes.

Now it was my turn to use my imagination.

* * *

Besides no food, patients received no medicine.

The "medicine" given to patients we called "rabbit shit" pills because that's what it looked like--brown and grainy and the size of rabbit waste. The ingredients were a mixture of herbs and rice dust. Rabbit shit pills were produced by the "revolutionary medical personnel," and administered for nearly every ailment.

Injectable medicines were stored in glass soda bottles--actual Coca-Cola or Seven-Up bottles. The bottle tops were wrapped with clear plastic and sealed with regular rubber bands. There were three colors: red, yellow, and clear. The red and yellow were vitamins and the clear ones were antibiotic, anti-fever, or simply "coconut juice."[8]

The "doctors" were "*pet komar*," or "child doctors." They ranged in age from barely ten-year-olds to teenagers. They dressed in clean black uniforms and wore the *krama* wrapped around their heads. Their dark skin reflected their pure Khmer background. *Child doctors* came from the peasant class, they were quick to say. In contrast, our lighter skin marked our "imperialist origins." Their skin was dark because they "worked hard under the sun," not like some of us with fairer skin, those of us who "never know what hard work is."

Child doctors were the ones directly involved in patient "care." They decided what oral medication the patients needed and what injectable medications needed to be given. The director of the hospital, a polite and apparently caring, *Mit* Peou, was not involved in the day-to-day care of patients. He was about my age, and, though he appeared to have received some education, never conducted "rounds" for the patients. The medical director's job was to work with the higher levels of *the organization* usually involving meetings outside the village, either local or regional.

Child doctors were also responsible for distributing rations to the patients--watery rice (you could barely see any grains of rice) and salt. Two of the *child doctors* carried a large container full of watery rice while another person ladled it onto the patient's plate. If a *child doctor* liked someone, he gave that person a little extra portion; if not, the person received even less to eat along with the admonition, "because you are too lazy." Once I saw a starving patient try to scoop rice from behind the backs of some *child*

---

[8] Once when I had suffered for two days from fever and chills with terrible shaking (I had no doubt in my mind it was malaria), I received coconut juice intravenously. To my utter amazement, I survived.

doctors. They beat him with a wooden stick and the flat side of one of the doctor's long knives.

*   *   *

But I didn't plan to come into this hospital to die. My goal had always been the same--to get close to the kitchen. Once I got to know a few of the kitchen workers and *child doctors*, I started collecting a few dead branches and dropping them off at the kitchen. Then I went back to my bed. As time passed, I noticed that when food was distributed, I received a bit extra because I was not "lazy."

The kitchen where the workers cooked rice or soup was built as an enclosed area so as to block the wind and speed up the cooking process. It had only one door and no windows. The main large pot was for cooking the watery rice, and the smaller pot was for soup (if there happened to be any vegetables like pumpkins, squashes, or even leaves). Most of the time, only the main stove was used. In the whole large pot only a few cans (14-ounce condensed milk cans) of rice was put in; the rest was all water. Once the water boiled, you could see a few grains of rice float to the top. There was a long-handled ladle next to the large pot. This was used to stir the rice from time to time to spread it evenly to avoid overcooked rice at the bottom of the pot. If you scooped the surface of the boiling porridge, you were likely to get only water with a few grains of rice. To get more rice you had to scoop deeper. Every time I brought in dry wood to feed the cooking fire, I looked around, and, if no one was looking at me, I scooped the rice while it was boiling. I slurped it as fast as I could before I got caught. I could feel the rush of heat as the water went down my throat. At first I developed plenty of blisters from burns in my mouth, but as time went on the lining of my mouth became more resistant to heat. Those days I thought if I somehow died it must be from my esophagus being burned. I figured that wouldn't be such a bad thing--dying with a full stomach was much better than dying of starvation. I did this day in and day out and never got caught. Only one person knew that I did this--A Da, a girl who was asked to help out in the kitchen because of her handicap--apparently polio. Not only did A Da ignore my stealing, she even served as lookout so I wouldn't be caught. With A Da's assistance, and the benefit of time,

I slowly gained some strength until, finally, I was able to help the *child doctors* with another of their jobs--collecting corpses.

The *child doctors* seemed happy for my help. After all, this was not a job any of them wanted, particularly when their title was *child doctor*. Every day, early in the morning, before sunrise, I helped prepare the trip, first by grabbing the two cows and securing them to the front of the cart. Then I helped collect the bodies and toss them onto the cart. Every day there were between ten and twenty bodies. At times, we had to make two trips because I couldn't load them all at once.

The place we dumped the bodies wasn't far from the hospital--about a quarter mile away. As the hospital was actually a cow barn, it sat on a patch of the farm's higher ground. You exited the hospital directly into farmland. One of the *child doctors* drove the oxcart, and I and two or three others walked behind.

I would help dig a pit to bury the bodies in. I dug a pit as best as I could, at times very shallow. Then we dumped the bodies, one by one, into the pit and covered them as best we could. After a while, I began to feel as if my own humanity was slipping away. I no longer felt I was dealing with human bodies, stiffened corpses. I felt as if they were merchandise, just objects. We got used to throwing them from the oxcart, like sacks of rice.

The next day, I repeated the task. Often, I found the bodies had been located by wild animals the night before and torn apart. Flies were everywhere.

Later, I learned that when you saw very green shrubbery or other thriving plants, it meant that bodies had been buried nearby. Until I learned this, I thought it was my lucky day if I found green, edible leaves. But once I learned this, I stayed away from all those vibrant, growing plants.

With these "volunteer" jobs, I was getting closer and closer to the kitchen. The *child doctors* liked my help, and they gave me extra rations. From time to time, I was asked to wash the pots and pans, and, gradually, I recovered my life. Subsequently, I became the "water carrier" as well as the "wood fetcher" for the hospital's kitchen. I was so glad I'd worked my way back to my old job.

A year or so later, because there had been so many deaths in the villages, the hospital was moved to a different location. A Da was moved out of the kitchen and directed to join the weavers group. At this second hospital, patients no longer had to sleep on the ground. Beds were set in long rows. The roof was new and had no holes, but there still weren't any walls, and patients still had to find bushes behind the "ward" in order to relieve themselves.

* * *

By this time I was somewhat recovered from starvation. I was slowly getting stronger. Then, one day, when my youngest sister, Sam Ang, who was 12-years-old, returned to the village. I convinced her to stay with me in the hospital.

I asked the vice director of the hospital, *Mit Neary* Reung, to allow Sam Ang to work in the kitchen. Surprisingly, or, perhaps not, my request was granted. By then I had a very good relationship with the staff and *Mit* Peov, the director and *Mit Neary* Reung. *Mit* Reung was a tall, beautiful girl with a lovely smile. She loved it when I told her how beautiful she was. Occasionally, I teased that she and *Mit* Peov made "a very good pair." I guess my objective of making myself useful to those who had power over me was paying off. By then, I'd been working in this "hospital" long enough to convince the Khmer Rouge that I was a very hard, dependable worker.

By this time, Mother could no longer care for herself, much less take care of her daughter, Sy, and so they both had become patients in the hospital. It felt like a family reunion. After one and a half years in the killing fields, we were the only four left alive. Mother suffered from severe generalized edema from malnourishment--everyone did. She was quite weak and couldn't walk far from her bed. One day I saw her urinate next to her bed. This wasn't healthy, and I scolded her. I was a fourth-year medical student, and I wanted her to practice preventive medicine. She listened, but I knew she wouldn't do what I told her. When you're weak, exhausted, and have swollen legs, you don't want to walk far to relieve yourself. I knew my advice was unrealistic (After all, hadn't I been handling feces with my bare hands?), but mother knew she couldn't survive much longer and, shortly after this, she passed away. Strangely, I can't remember how I buried her. I just simply cannot remember. To this day, I ask myself how I could forget this. I was no longer involved in helping move the dead.

After the Khmer Rouge cut off Sy's food ration, she weakened even further. She had tried everything she was advised to try--from applications of fruit or tree salves to crushed, burned frog, but the wound wouldn't heal. One day while I was with her she handed me a pendant our mother had left her. She asked me to keep it. "I don't want my body to be disturbed by the people around me," she said. Often, even before a patient died, another patient would strip the dying of anything useful or of value--from jewelry to such simple items as a spoon, hammock, or kettle--even the clothes a person was wearing. Sy had witnessed this every day. She knew her time was coming and wanted to be sure I had the pendant before her death.

I can't recall how I buried my sister either.

* * *

I returned to the position of "water carrier" for the hospital, though in the new hospital the water source was too far away to go on foot. Every morning before sunrise I grabbed two cows and yoked them to the oxcart. I put the bamboo yoke and two metal buckets on the cart's side rail. The water storage tank was nothing but an old 55-gallon steel gasoline drum laid horizontally in the middle of the cart. I climbed up to the front of the cart and with a small branch in my hand I urged the cows forward. Off I went to get water.

Dressed in faded peasant clothes with a *krama* wrapped around my neck, I felt like a typical Khmer peasant. (No one called me Chinese here.) Driving an oxcart along a dirt road to fetch water was the best job I could have. The road was essentially empty. Occasionally, a soldier on his bicycle might pass by, but most of the time I was the only one on the road. Shade trees bordered the dirt road on both sides. The only sounds I could hear were the tree leaves rustling in the breeze and the squeaking of the oxcart's wheels. It was these comforting sounds that submerged me into the tranquility of nature.

At such times I reflected on my past life. Things had changed so much in just a couple of years. No school, no stethoscope, no white coat, no hospital rotation, no friends to share stories and no family to share thoughts with. Instead of a pen to write with, now I held a branch in my hand to maneuver the cows. Now my prized possession was a spoon. I remembered what my grandfather used to tell me was a precept of Buddhism, "to agree with what you have and what you are." I had to accept what I was given. At the same time, I felt thankful that I'd survived living on the edge of starvation.

From time to time I steered the cows around a deep hole or rut. Sometimes I simply hummed old songs I knew. The one I liked the most was "*Sayon Toch Yum*" ("The Cry of Gibbons in the Afternoon") by Sin Sisamouth. It was a classic song about being separated from loved ones:

> *Others are separated for only one day*
> *They cry out loud*
> *But as for me*
> *The earth will turn around ten times*
> *And still I will never meet them again*
> *Dear God, please help untie the knot*
> *And free me from sufferings*
> *So I no longer worry*
>
> *And I cried. Alone.*

My partners preferred to go into the forest to collect dead branches for the kitchen because such work gave them an opportunity to search for edible things, but I preferred to stick with the solitary job of fetching water. This way I could shed my tears and sorrows and no one knew.

* * *

The worst incident I witnessed while working in this new hospital was the body of a young man cut into pieces by other patients. This young man was sent here after he was no longer able to work in the rice field. On his arrival, he was already motionless. He was breathing, but couldn't eat. The next night he died. In the middle of the night, a dispute broke out among a group of patients. In the quiet of the night, the clamor drew the attention of the *child doctors*. Once the Khmer Rouge learned that the patients had been arguing about "unequal shares" of the meat, they were told to gather around the pot and fill their stomachs. The *child doctors* wanted to prove these patients were not human. "Humans do not eat humans," they said.

As directed, the patients sat around the pot and continued choosing pieces of meat, all the while knowing full well that this was their last meal.

Anything done against the Khmer Rouge's "revolutionary wheel" was considered against the law. It did not matter how small or unintentional--stealing commune food, leaving work to search for food--any of these and a host of other infractions could mark you as an enemy of the state. The Khmer Rouge often told us, "We have no prisons, no shackles or chains to bind you. We use a simple thread, but a thread so strong you dare not break it."

In this case, the law was in the hands of a few *child doctors*, teenagers.

That same night, in the middle of the night, those patients were told to step up onto the oxcart. Then all of them were taken away and put to death.

* * *

By the end of 1977, I'd lost everything. Starvation had claimed the lives of my family, one by one, until only my youngest sister, Sam Ang, and I survived. Not only were we still alive, but, actually, relatively healthy. At least, we weren't starving the way other patients were. And our work wasn't as laborious as that of many others. But after mother and Sy died, Sam Ang was no longer interested in remaining in the hospital. She didn't like to be near the *child doctors*.

One night, not long after Sy's death, I heard Sam Ang crying. She was sitting on one of the long logs scattered about the clearing of the Khmer Rouge hospital. I sat down in the dark next to her. A few moments later, her words reached out in an uncertain voice.

"*Bang* (brother), I don't want to stay here," she said and began crying again.

I loved this girl very much. My mother, with her last words, had asked me to take care of Sam Ang. Mother believed that in the future only me and Sam Ang would have a chance to survive, and, undoubtedly, I would become the father of my sister. I was the one who had begged the head of the hospital to give her a place to live, to let her work next to me since I knew that nowhere else could she get more food than here. I served as "water carrier" and "wood fetcher," and she washed dishes, cleaned up around the kitchen, and helped prepare food for the Khmer Rouge *child doctors*. Many times, she told me how unhappy she was in the "hospital." I knew how difficult it was for Sam Ang to work so near the Khmer Rouge.

They never failed to remind us of our lowly status as *new people*. Sam Ang said she could no longer bear the words they used toward her. I couldn't blame her. I understood that her burden was a heavy one.

She was isolated from other children and didn't feel she belonged with the Khmer Rouge *child doctors*. She preferred to associate with the children of *new people* and believed she more properly belonged with the group of children working in the canals outside and distant from the village. This labor group moved around from place to place and hardly ever returned to the village. She knew that the labor was definitely harder, but she liked the fact that everyone worked hard. Here, at the "hospital," she felt she was the only one who worked; she was the only one who had to please all the *child doctors*. She just didn't feel comfortable.

Sam Ang rested her head on my shoulder. I combed her close-cropped, raven hair with my fingers. I knew that in the labor group, she'd likely be given more, or at least enough, food to survive. I also knew she had already made her decision, and I could feel this was probably my last chance to be with her. I didn't want her to be out of my sight. I tried to convince her that in the near future, the system would change.

"It won't always be like this," I said.

She nodded and went back to her hammock.

The next morning, I was ordered to leave the hospital. I was shocked. *Mit* Peou, the head of the hospital (likely a high school graduate), told me an order "from the top" directed me to join the carpentry group.

Stunned, I stood stock still. I thought of Mother's last words.

What about Sam Ang?

I asked *Mit* Peou if he could keep my sister working in the hospital.

"For now, I plan to keep her here," he said.

That same day I was relocated to Cham Ro Ar. I didn't even have a chance to tell Sam Ang goodbye because she'd left earlier that morning to fetch rice from the next village.

With my departure, each of us was now alone.

Chapter 7

In 1978, internal purges caused upheaval in the Khmer Rouge political party. The Khmer Rouge split into eight sections according to the points of the compass. For instance, if they came from the East side of Cambodia, they called themselves the "East" side. With eight directions there were eight divisions: East, West, North, South, and then the Northeast, Southeast, Southwest, and Northwest.[9] Khmer Rouge from *Peayorb*, the Northwest, arrived in Svay Chhrum and started to eliminate the then current village division. Except for the medical director, *Mit* Poeu, they installed new chiefs in all the various departments. We *new people* were told that this was the new direction from a higher level of *the organization*. When this power switch occurred, there was no resistance and no fighting. It was a very quiet transfer of power. One day, we suddenly saw new Khmer Rouge cadre in the village. Older leaders simply "transferred out of the area" or just were no longer there. No extra soldiers appeared. There was no resistance. It was just a quiet, deadly silent replacement.[10] Without resistance, the older groups were led out of the village. Their fate wasn't known to us for certain, but everyone guessed they were simply eliminated.[11]

Shortly after this transfer of power, *Angkar* began looking for people

---

[9] The Eastern zone remained largely unaffected by the internal purge until May 1978 when So Phim led a revolt that provoked massive retaliation by Pol Pot's Southwestern henchmen. As many as 100,000 people in the Eastern zone--labeled people with "Khmer bodies but Vietnamese minds"--were liquidated or deported to other parts of the country to face certain death.

[10] I strongly believe that the way the Khmer Rouge structured their organization was both powerful and successful. The repeated speeches and indoctrination, whether for the *old* or the *new people*, were so intimidating that no one dared disagree with *Angkar's* direction. If *Angkar* told you what to do, you just didn't argue with it.

[11] This coincided with the Khmer Rouge's poor relationship with Vietnam and had something to do with Vietnamese support of the internal resistance to the Pol Pot regime. And the purge was started from the very top--Hu Nim, the very prominent minister of information.

who might be related to the Vietnamese (including the Khmer who came from Kampuchea Krom[12]) either by name or history (or even speaking with Vietnamese accent) and "eliminated" all of them. One of these victims was *Ta* Yeh, member of my water supply team in the "new" hospital. The Khmer Rouge took his whole family away.[13]

It was soon after this power grabs that, all of a sudden, *Mit* Peou told me he was no longer able to keep me around. "You're too healthy to be in the hospital," he said.

I knew if it were in his power to keep me, he would. I didn't know for certain how educated he was, but I guessed he was probably a high school graduate, or at least nearly so. My relationship with *Mit* Peou was sound, so much so that I eventually shared part of my previous life with him. He knew, for example, that I was a fourth-year medical student. I considered myself lucky to meet him. Whenever the hospital kitchen had some leftovers, he told the *child doctors* to bring them to me. One day I received a piece of crunchy rice from him. It was the overdone, crispy layer of rice that stuck to the bottom of the pot. Coated with palm sugar, it was so sweet I felt as if I was in heaven.

I remember one occasion when the two of us, along with several other hospital staffers, had gone to the river to get fish and clams for the kitchen. It was an overnight trip made with two oxcarts. I was the only *new person* allowed to go with them. We went to a riverbank on the other side of Highway 5. It took us only a little more than half a day to reach the river. Once we arrived, I saw a world that was so different from the one I knew. The sand on the riverbank was as white and fine just as beach sand. It was the first time I'd seen a clear water since I'd left the city. I had been barefoot in this regime for almost three years by that time, and the soles of my feet

---

[12] Ethnic Khmer who lived in Kampuchea Krom, an area in southern Vietnam that was once part of the Khmer Empire. They spoke Khmer with a Vietnamese accent and thus were collectively considered by the Khmer Rouge as "Vietnamese."

[13] When I looked at the overwhelming numbers of the *new people* coming to this region, we outnumbered the Khmer Rouge by no less than 100 to 1. With the ways the Khmer Rouge killed people, with the way they used the illiterates to "hold" us, with the way they repeated their messages everyday, with the way they reminded us "not to put our hands or legs against the wheel," we just succumbed to our own fragile demise by not daring to fight for our own survival.

were thicker and stronger. The heat, small thorns, rocks, and slippery dirt--they didn't bother me now, and I could still feel the fineness of the sand. I felt like a kid again as I watched my footprints form behind me. Clams here were so abundant we filled large pots with them in practically no time. We were warned, however, not to collect too many. The clams were only for the medical staff, not the patients. I was allowed to eat with them. They'd brought soy sauce along with them, and the taste of the cooked clams and soy sauce was beyond my imagination. I could eat all the clams I wanted.

For a moment I forgot about my past, but later I thought of Vimol, my son, who had cried because he didn't receive a portion of soy sauce. Why did they allow thousands of us to die when such an abundant food source existed only one day away by oxcart from our village?

The water here was so clear because the place was undisturbed by humans. No one was here except us. None of my family had the chance I had. It was also the only time I got the chance to take a bath in clear, clean water. I even washed the cows in this water, just as Khmer villagers would care for their animals. In the village we never could wash the cows because we had no water. The only time the cows got washed was when it rained.

Next to the riverbank sat a small house. It was of the old style and untouched by the war. All of us stayed there that night. I was resting in my hammock very close to *Mit* Peou. (Usually *new people* were not allowed to sleep in the same area as *old people*.) My eyes were closed, but I wasn't asleep. It was then that I overheard him listening to the Voice of America. After a few short moments, he hurriedly turned it off. I pretended not to notice and said nothing. We returned the next day.

Now *Mit* Peou told me he would recommend me to the carpentry group in a village called Cham Ro Ar, which was under the supervision of one of his comrades, Achar Po. The day I left Svay Chhrum, I thanked *Mit* Peou for giving me and my sister, Sam Ang, a place to live. Chom Ro Ar was only about two or three miles back in the direction of Highway 5. It was on the same road that our family was forced to pass after we were dropped off the military trucks so long ago. We'd passed through this place before arriving in Svay Chhrum. I don't believe the population here was more than a thousand. With every step toward Cham Ro Ar, Mother's last words echoed in my head. I kept wishing I'd had a chance to say goodbye to Sam Ang. I was so afraid I might not see her again.

When I arrived in Cham Ro Ar, I handed *Mit* Peou's letter to Achar Po and began my life as a carpenter.

* * *

I didn't know the first thing about carpentry, but as I arrived, I saw a group of about twenty men; two were sawing wood. This doesn't look too hard to learn, I thought, and so I told the Khmer Rouge I could saw wood.

As it happens, sawing wood proved to be quite a challenging job for me, at least at the beginning. I found I had a lot to learn about this work. For one, you need to get the sawteeth as sharp as possible; that way you use less energy to saw.

The wood came to us in large pieces--actual tree trunks. Three persons were responsible for sawing wood. Two were *new people*; I was one of them. The third person was *Mit* Rom, one of the *old people*, and the leader of our group of sawyers. The other group of about a dozen men planed the wood. The two main carpenters were *Mit* Kun and *Ta* Khim.

The bark had already been shaved off the tree trunks before being transported down to Cham Ro Ar from a mountain village called Sdok Proveuk. My job was to saw the log into assigned sizes--4 x 4, 3 x 4, and so on. I had to place the log onto stands, mark the top part of the wood with charcoal lines, and then saw it following the mark.

It wasn't that hard to saw it straight from the top because I could see the lines. However, I was standing on that large piece of wood, and I couldn't see the bottom while I was sawing. If the log was tilted or my position was a little off center, or my saw wasn't sharp, there was a good possibility my bottom cut wouldn't be straight. I remember once when one of the Khmer Rouge chiefs called me "an enemy of the state" because I'd failed to saw a log straight down to the bottom. In those days, the Khmer Rouge talked very highly of what they called "merit." But no matter how hard you worked or how strong your spirit and mind was in following the revolution, no matter what our "merits," we, *new people*, just simply could never reach their status. Any mistake we made, however slight or unintentional, was considered an attempt to oppose the revolution. It could mark us as "enemies of the people."

Day by day, I perfected my skills, though. Living and working with the best carpenters provided me great learning opportunities. When I was a boy, I'd watched my grandfather sharpen knives and wanted to learn how, but was told I was too young to learn. Maybe he feared I'd ruin his knives. Anyway, I wished I'd learned those skills earlier. I came to learn that in carpentry, the key to success is knowing how to sharpen your tools. It didn't matter if it was a saw blade or a plane blade, when it was sharp, my work would definitely be easier--and, very importantly, I used less energy.

Living conditions here were somewhat better. Our commune hut was a long hall with a roof tall enough so that we no longer had to bend over to enter. And there were walls, so we no longer feared the rain.

As the days passed, I learned plenty of skills from the carpenter, *Ta Khim*. I even built my own bed. I carved a rising sun on the headboard to give me hope that someday I would be out of this place, and I could live to see real sunshine again. Some of the others made cots designed for mobility by using rice sacks for cloth. When it was hot, they would move their cots outside to sleep. All in all, compared to my previous work, it was wonderful to be in the carpentry group.

Though the sleeping area was improved, our belongings were still as meager as ever--two pairs of clothes, a *krama*, a spoon, a hammock, and a sheet cover all stowed in a "*sac a dos*" (a French term for "backpack"). Every time we went off to work, we left our *sac a dos* in the commune sleeping area.

But my *sac a dos* contained something else, something none of the others had--mine contained a new pair of sandals I'd made for Sam Ang.

* * *

The revolution had now taken "one step forward" we were told, and *Angkar* gave us new direction. To improve our living standards, we carpenters were to build houses for the people. Each new all-wooden house would be two stories as in the old days. It sat on high posts set over cement supports and had a stairway leading to the front porch. Double doors would lead into the main room. The floor would be all wood. The windows would have blinds. Each family was to have a house. The location already was selected. The houses would be built along a straight line running through the village. For now, just one row.

Families would not be permitted to move into the new houses, however, until all the houses were completed. According to the Khmer Rouge, to allow one family to move in before others violated revolutionary concept because if one family lived in a new house and the others didn't, then we wouldn't be "equal."

* * *

Acha Po, the chief of the whole center, was in his mid forties. Everyone knew that he was a former diplomat from a Buddhist society, and this made him the most educated Khmer Rouge chief in this region. His speech and manners clearly reflected his education. His fair complexion belied his unlikely background as pure Khmer. I hardly ever saw him in the rice fields, and I never saw him near the buffalos. He was, however, knowledgeable about carpentry. Acha Po had a wife and two sons. The older one, named Kra, was eight years old. Acha Po smiled openly and seemed sincere, but was very firm in giving directions. No one, not even the *old people*, dared dispute his suggestions.

The Khmer Rouge took charge of all aspects of our lives, including the choice of a marriage partner. They conducted mass weddings--twenty to fifty couples at a time. Couples were directed to live separately with their respective work team until *Angkar* directed them to meet again. Women began searching for an appropriate partner so as to avoid a forced marriage. I saw two young girls hang themselves side by side from the top of a tree because they couldn't accept the Khmer Rouge-arranged partners.

I was determined to avoid marriage as long as possible; I saw no reason for it. Nonetheless, in the event Acha Po forced me to marry someone, I had mentally "chosen" a particular young girl (though we never spoke about a relationship). This girl eventually chose to marry a fisherman who I was sure could provide her with extra food. I could not blame her.[14]

* * *

For easy access in wood loading, the carpenters' workshop was located next to the main road. It was divided into three separate areas: the sawing area, the wood-planing area, and a large wood storage room.

---

[14] I was one of only two men in our village who was able to avoid a forced Khmer Rouge marriage. The UN-backed tribunal investigating Khmer Rouge mass killings and other brutalities has also turned to investigating forced marriage. Between 1975 and 1979, prosecutors estimate several hundred thousand people were "married" in Khmer Rouge "ceremonies."

In the sawing area there was a large pole set horizontally on two giant legs, each of which was formed of two large, waist-high logs that crossed to form an "X" with the socket serving to house and immobilize the horizontal pole. The horizontal log was long enough to accommodate three people. The back ends of the large tree trunks that were brought in from the mountain forest to be sawn were balanced on a horizontal beam with its front end resting on a movable support bar. Once your cut line hit the support bar below, you moved to the ground below and used your back to lift the tree trunk which allowed you to move the support bar back to the front so you could continue sawing. (The tree trunk sat on the horizontal bar so even though it was very heavy you still could lift the front end with your back.)

The saw frame was constructed of three pieces of bamboo so as to make it light. The blade was held between the two short bars on one side. The vertical long piece of bamboo sat parallel to the blade. To tighten the blade, a wire was used to tighten the opposite side of the short bars. The saw was as high as my chin. You could saw wood in a one- or two-person style. One person held the string on one end. The string was coated with wet charcoal powder. Another person pulled the string all the way to the front and pulled it tight. He lifted the string and snapped it back on the wood, making a black line. To saw, you stood on the wood, set your sawteeth on the charcoal line, and sawed it by balancing your two hands on the top bar. The hardest part was to get the sawteeth to catch the face of the wood. To do that you had to place your saw perpendicular to the front end, then move it up and down. Once your sawteeth caught the wood, you inclined the saw to a 45-degree angle and used a push--pull motion to saw.

When I first began work as a sawyer, I found myself pushing and pulling faster than *Mit* Rom, and yet I still couldn't catch up with him. At first, I thought it was only because I was new to the work. *Mit* Rom sharpened his saw twice a day. I didn't know how to sharpen the saw, and I thought if I continued sawing while *Mit* Rom took his break to sharpen his saw, I would catch him up with him someday, especially once I'd perfected my arm motion. Still, I couldn't catch up with *Mit* Rom. I began to accept that it must be the sharpening. I looked to see how different *Mit* Rom's sawteeth were, and after I watched him for a while, I tried to practice sharpening the saw during the break. Once I knew this secret, I became as good as *Mit* Rom. And I learned that when your saw was sharp, the sound it produced was crisp, and the dust that came off the saw was coarser. And, importantly, with one stroke you could actually see the saw advancing. You used less force and saved a lot of energy.

This also held true when planing wood. At night, we didn't saw wood; we planed it. You had to know how to sharpen the blade, and you had to know how to adjust the length of the blade from the plane's surface. If your blade wasn't sharp or extended too far, you couldn't plane wood smoothly. The plane frequently jammed in the wood, and blisters formed on your hand.

* * *

In a whole year, we carpenters managed to build thirteen houses. If we had just 500 families in the village it would take us more than thirty years to build enough houses for everyone. It would be just as long, more than thirty years, before people would be allowed to live in these *modern* houses. After we finished building all these houses, no one was allowed to live in them, and you couldn't live in one anyway because no house had a roof yet.

What an "immense, marvelous, miraculous, supreme, grand, luminous" idea of Angkar! I thought.

* * *

In the end, only two people were selected to remain on the support bar to saw wood during the beginning of the rice-planting season, June through September, and during harvest, December to February. And I was one of them! While others were mobilized to labor in the rice fields, I stayed on the wood stack day in and day out. Though I was frequently sent to saw wood at a recently built house, essentially, I was on my own. My job was "to lift and drop" the saw all day long. I eventually became so skilled that I was assigned to saw wood into window blinds--very thin cuts. By that time, I'd become a very trusted person in terms of being "the owner of my duty," and the Khmer Rouge could judge me by looking at the quantity and quality of my work products. I was always working in a place that was dry. It didn't matter if I was at the base or at a house, I always stayed dry and never had to deal with mud in the rice fields. Staying in dry places prevented me from suffering any cut in the muddy fields that might lead to leg infections, the very problem that led to the deaths of Chin Hor and my sister, Sy.

And that was how I survived.

* * *

Living and working in Cham Ro Ar, I'd come to know Acha Po, the Khmer Rouge Carpentry Supervisor and chief of the community center.

During rest or lunch breaks, while others went out looking for insects, crabs, snakes, or other things to eat, I kept working with wood. This "volunteer work" fit into my plan. I built things like a "Peuy Ee" frame, a folding cot made from two bars of wood with four legs. Sometimes I'd construct a wooden bed for the *old people* out of scrap lumber and even make a crutch for an amputee. In this way, I made myself visible as a person who worked all the time--unlike most others who were preoccupied with searching for food. I also was given access to Acha Po's home though I never dared to steal food or anything else from his house.

Starvation is a powerful force. It can lead a person to risk his life to calm his stomach. So many were caught and killed. In those times, a Khmer Rouge song claimed "a small bag is a decent possession." One day Acha Po asked me, "Do you know what 'a small bag' refers to?" Before I could answer he said, "It is your stomach, the small bag within you. It's your only decent possession." But I asked myself if this was the only possession I should have, then why would *Angkar* deprive us from filling this small bag? We were asked to abandon everything in our previous lives and were deprived of everything, our families included, and yet it was still not enough.

In any case, I earned the trust of Acha Po. I did it by not searching for food during breaks. He even allowed me to lead his 8-year-old son, Kra, back to the village from the mountain. Kra was staying with his mother, Acha Po's wife, in Sdok Proveuk, the mountain village where the trees were cut. My assignment was to hike up there and bring his boy back to Cham Ro Ar. Obviously this was a job I wanted. There was no work for me except to walk up to Sdok Proveuk by myself with rice I carried for me alone. The walk up there took all day. For our return the next day, Achar Po's wife loaded us with enough rice and food for the two of us. I felt like

I was on vacation. Besides having this food, I only needed to carry Kra a few times. He was old enough to walk by himself except for a few times when he was tired.

Even though I didn't make it a practice to search for food during breaks, I was still hungry all the time. It's beyond words, how much a starving person can eat if he's allowed to. (A friend of mine once ate a whole box of rice he cooked in a discarded M16 ammunition case.) One day as I walked past my old village, Svay Chhum, site of the "hospital." I went in to the place where they produced sugar from palm juice. I asked the responsible chief, whom I knew back then, for a piece of sugar. Sugar was so hard to find in those days. He allowed me to enter the storage room and eat as much as I could. The sugar was still in a liquid state. I gorged myself, downing thirteen ladles before I found myself so stuffed I couldn't possibly drink any more.

Afterward, I ambled back to Cham Ro Ar, all the while feeling how lucky I was to get this much sugar into my body. At that time, I lived on the second floor of a recently built house. By *Angkar* direction, no one was permitted to move into a new house until "all the houses" were completely finished. But we, as carpenters, could stay there because it was our job to build the houses. My place was on the second floor at a back corner. That night, by the time I got to my place, it was almost dark, and I didn't feel comfortable at all. My stomach was so full. We used to joke about the feeling of being too full: You couldn't lie down, you couldn't sit, and you couldn't walk. That night, I felt what it is to be unable to sit still. I could feel the heat generated by the glucose inside my stomach. I felt nauseated, but tried not to vomit. This was a very special treat, thirteen ladles of plain sugar. *This is never going to happen again in my life*, I thought. I propped myself up on a wooden handrail in the hope that gravity would hold that precious sugar in place. I strongly believed at that time that if I could hold this sugar in, I would feel better later that night or, at least, by morning. But, after a while, no matter what I tried, I couldn't hold it any longer. I thought I could rush downstairs to vomit, but the urge was unstoppable. I projectile vomited from the top floor. Luckily no one was there to see this. I had to scramble down outside to bury my vomit so the sugar smell wouldn't be detected. I felt so much better afterward but couldn't believe I couldn't save this precious thing. Not only did I lose all of that valuable sugar, but I had to hurry to bury my vomit so no one would know that it was plain sugar. Otherwise, I could be accused of stealing sugar, a claim that could mean my death.

*   *   *

The village of Cham Ro Ar had a blacksmith shop. Four or five people worked there. One of them, *Ta* Mak, one of the *old people*, was still married in his 60's, but blind in both eyes. His job was to push and pull the large bellows for the charcoal oven. Well-known for his cockiness, he liked to brag about his ability to travel without getting lost despite being sightless. The others were real ironworkers; they looked very healthy and muscular. They made tools like knives, sickles, hoes, hatchets and axes as well as larger nails, and so on.

If you knew someone who worked there, you could arrange to have personal items made--like spoons. That was one thing I always carried in my pocket--a spoon. Instead of carrying a pen or keys like I did during peacetime, I now carried a spoon. Definitely a necessity in those times, it became one of my most valuable possessions. Anyone who lost his spoon was in trouble. Some of us would cheat by designing our own spoon, for example, a spoon with a larger bowl. Our ration of watery rice, or on rare occasions, plain rice, was distributed in portions of ten. Usually, we apportioned the rice among us in equal shares. But, we couldn't divide soup into ten parts because the amount was too small, so whoever had a bigger spoon had an advantage. Some people even bent their spoons close to a 90-degree angle so they'd be able to more easily scoop up the soup at the bottom of the soup bowl. Everyone was hungry--all the time.

As you approached the smithy, you could hear the loud clang of two blacksmiths' hammers, alternating hammering into shape whatever their project was.

I had a beautiful hatchet made here. With the skill I'd acquired as a carpenter, I fashioned its handle from the spoke of an oxcart wheel. In those days, road conditions were poor so wheel spokes were of a strong, black wood called "*kra nhoung*." I sharpened my hatchet almost daily to make sure it stayed sharp and bright. Every day I carried it to work by wrapping a *krama* around my waist as a belt and inserting the hatchet at my right side.

It was at the smithy that I found time to make a pair of sandals from a rubber tire. I got along well with my leader, *Mit* Rom, and he gave me four pieces of automobile tire and even taught me how to make sandals. You need a very sharp, strong knife to cut a tire into the shape of a shoe. It took a lot of work and hand strength to make a clean cut as the tire was quite thick. Then, again with a strong, sharp, but smaller blade you made four through cuts in the front and two in the back to hold the tire tube that was used for the sandal straps. You then passed a thin tweezers through the bottom cut and inserted the tire tube end piece that as precut for the strap and then pulled it out through the sandal's base. It wasn't that easy for me to do. The straps were then secured without any glue. After I finished, I kept these sandals in my *sac a dos* at all times and waited in the hope that someday I would get a chance to present them to my sister, Sam Ang.

* * *

One day, while I was at work, someone stole another person's tobacco. Acha Po and his team entered our sleeping area and began searching through every single personal bag. It was then that Acha Po found both my medical school ID and the ID picture of my father. For nearly three years, these were the two most important items I had hidden in my *sac a dos*. These were the only two pictures I still possessed. (I also had my mother's pendant, but I carried this on my person at all times.) I thought someday I might return to Phnom Penh, and (who knows?) I might even be able to return to medical school. My medical school ID was the only proof I had that I'd once been a medical student. It wasn't until the next day that I found out that this search for stolen tobacco had been conducted.

Since my father's death, I'd kept his ID picture with me. My father had become an orphan before he even started school. I hardly knew my grandparents on my father's side. I never even saw a picture of them. All I know is that they were very poor. Father was born in Kean Klaing, which was situated next to Chhroy Changva, just across the river from the capital, Phnom Penh. I visited his birthplace a few times. In those days, the late 50s and early 60s, there was no bridge. We had to cross by boat. As a child, I loved to ride the boat. As you approached the dock you heard the boat horn. The large exhaust pipe in the middle of the boat sent out trails of smoke that faded into the sky. It was just peaceful to look at. It was a short ride. The distance across the river was only about 1500 feet, depending on the season, but the sights and the air were breathtaking. Once you reached the other side, you walked up the dock, and as soon as you set foot on shore, you saw three or four waiting horse carts along with a few "*romok*," a cart that was pulled behind a bicycle. In Cambodia, *romok* were everywhere--in Phnom Penh and my birthplace--but as far as I remember, you had to go to Chhroy Changva to see horse carts. The horse-drawn cart was wider and larger than the *romok*. It sat on two automobile tires and bounced more than the *romok*. Each horse wore blinders and was decorated with flowers or multicolored material on its head to attract customers. Once you climbed onto the cart, you heard the whinny of the horse, and as it galloped along, it threw up a small dust cloud behind. It was a slow ride along a winding road flanked by small houses. There were no paved roads, just dirt lanes. Tree leaves rustling in the river breeze made the ride even more peaceful. The houses always had a few trees in front that provided shade for small vendors. Some households set a small urn of water beside the front gate for the benefit of thirsty foot travelers. Everyone knew everyone, and you could hear the villagers shouting out to you from the street or house, "Coming to visit?" I have only a vague memory of the house--the floor was made of bamboo that was split in half with the rounded side forming the floor.

My father had been adopted by an older couple I knew as "grandpa" and "grandma." My father never told me the story of his birth parents. He was just too busy working. His adoptive parents took him to Prek Pnov, my birthplace, about 12 kilometers west of Phnom Penh on Highway 5. They sent him to school when he was young, but he only had the chance to attend school for a few years. (It was the same school I attended as a boy.) Initially, he helped out in the family grocery store. Later on, he transported palm sugar to Vietnam by canoe. He received no income from his work, only food and housing. I remember asking him about this once. He answered that his adoptive parents loved him and taught him about life, and that was all he cared about. He married my mother when she was about 15- or 16-years old. It was an arranged marriage.

My parents moved to Phnom Penh when I was six and started their own business, a small grocery store. My father tried to teach me since I was quite young what it meant to be a merchant: "You have to be friendly and sincere and willing to deliver merchandise to a customer's home free of charge."

In the midst of his success with the grocery, a fire destroyed our entire block, and we had to start life anew. I was only 7- or 8-years-old at the time. Father lost everything, and yet he had to raise me and my sisters.

One of my father's distant relatives worked for the government as a provincial forestry chief, a more comfortable way of life than ours. "That's all right," my father used to say. "We just weren't meant to be rich. " He said if he had been given the chance to go to school, he wouldn't have become a grocer. That was probably why he would do anything to get me through school.

As a child, I used to wish I'd been born to a government official rather than a grocery store owner. But later I began to appreciate my father's strength. He had little formal schooling, yet he had a good understanding of business. He taught me an old saying, *"tok tok penh bampong."* It means that one drop at a time can fill a container in the same way a farmer collects palm juice. Every morning the farmer climbs the palm tree to place bamboo containers under the shaved palm flowers. The next morning he returns to collect the containers filled with palm juice.

Every time I rode father's Vespa with him through the city streets, he would quiz me on the street names. Riding the Vespa with Father to pick up merchandise for the store was one of the few free times we spent together. As a young child, I stood in that open space in the middle of the Vespa, and he would test me on the street names. He tried to teach me as best he could.

I'd kept my father's picture hidden in my bag because I missed him.

* * *

That day, the Cham Ro Ar tobacco thief was not found. In the commune meeting the day after he'd conducted his search, Acha Po reminded us that "In our revolutionary era there should not be any thieves. Stealing was part of the old imperialist society. It doesn't belong in our current bright and equal revolution. Stealing is forbidden, and if the thief is caught you all know what *Angkar* will do.

I've also discovered that some of you are still attached to family sentiments. You're still not able to completely drop this mentality as *Angkar* directs."

He didn't mention finding the pictures in my sac a dos, and he didn't mention my name, but I knew he was talking about me. The message was clear.

Later, we stood outside, just Achar Po and me, next to his small house about 200 feet from our commune hut. He had taken me aside.

He warned me I should not keep anything that reminded me of the old regime.

"You aren't yet ready to abandon your past," he said. (In other words, I hadn't yet been successfully brainwashed by the revolution.)

By then I felt very close to Acha Po. I felt no apprehension standing alone next to him at that moment. The fact that this had happened and I wasn't immediately called in made me think I likely would be spared. He didn't appear upset or agitated. The way he conversed with me reminded me of how a father guides his son about right and wrong. I sensed he was trying to protect me rather than condemn me for "wrongdoing." I stood there silently beside him as if I was trying to absorb "his advice." At the same time, I felt thankful for the special bond and friendship I shared with him.

This private encounter with Acha Po did give me pause though. On one hand, I knew I should listen to him to avoid punishment and possibly death. But that meant giving up my father's picture, a picture so dear to me. It was the only picture I had of anyone in my family. It represented my past. I had to make a quick decision, while the picture was probably still in Acha Po's house, otherwise I would never see my father's picture again.

Later that day, during the work break when Acha Po was likely out of the house, I cautiously made my way up the four ladder stairs of his house. With his wife away in Sdok Proveuk, most of time he lived here alone. I'd been here many times. His house was small, just like the rest of the houses of the *old people*. There was no private kitchen. There was no furniture, no pictures hung on the bare walls.

And, there, beside the single door, I saw both pictures lying on the floor. And I took my father's picture back.[15] Because I still feared Acha Po, I left my medical school ID untouched.

Then I waited for a reaction from Acha Po, praying he wouldn't harm me when he found out what I'd done, yet knowing in my heart that he wouldn't kill me. The next day, and in the days following, Acha Po acted as if nothing had happened. I'd survived to continue my labors. Still, I felt certain that if any other person had done what I had done, Acha Po would have killed him.

* * *

About a month after I'd begun life as a carpenter in Cham Ro Ar, word reached me that my sister, Sam Ang, had left her work at the "hospital" and joined the teenager group laboring in the rice fields. I knew this would happen soon or later. Sam Ang had been unhappy working so near the *child doctors* in the "hospital." I didn't know what I could or should do, but *left the problem to the spirit of my mother.* I just wished I had been there when she left so I could at least have said goodbye.

In the meantime, I'd kept the rubber sandals I'd made for Sam Ang in the hope that I would see her again someday.

. . . And then, one day, I did.

* * *

One day, my close friend, *Mit* An, and I were sitting on a roof support of one of the new houses. We were nailing the supports to the frames. I remember An asking me what was in my mind as I stared out to the horizon as I so often did while we were on the roof. I answered by asking him when he thought we could get out of this world.

He just smiled a wry smile as if to say, "Not a chance."

It was then that I caught sight of a long line of young *"neary"* (a team of girls) walking toward us along the road beside the house. My heart

---

[15] This was the only picture I managed to bring with me out of the killing fields. It now commands a place of honor in our home for our children to look at. I lost all the pictures of my childhood and all other pictures of my family. With that, I suppose, in some way, I lost my past.

started pounding. Could this be my sister's labor group? I hurried down off the roof and dashed to the roadside. I eagerly searched the face of each girl as she passed by. And. . .there! In the middle of the long line of girls, I spotted her! Sam Ang! Like all the other girls, she was dressed in black. I never thought I'd see her again. She smiled as she ran toward me. I also ran to her. My tears of joy rushed out faster than words.

Before I could say anything else, I said, "Wait! I have a gift for you!"

I dashed to my commune hut, pulled the sandals from my *sac a dos* and ran back to her. Not many words passed between us, but I could see Sam Ang was happy. I hadn't seen her this happy since before mother's death. She wasn't crying like me. She still looked to be in good health. She was only 14 or 15-years-old then. She wore the face of an angel. Her cheeks were still full; she wasn't starving.

Thankfully, the line of *neary* was a long one. Still, she could stay with me only a few short moments. There were no questions about other family members. By this time we were the only two survivors of our family. I knew deep down that she was also happy to see me but she was not as emotional as I was. The sandals I'd made for her were important to me. I knew they would protect her feet, one the best ways to remain healthy in those days. To get to see her again, to know she was healthy, was beyond anything I could ask for.

I handed her the sandals. She slipped them on right away. They fit perfectly. She smiled.

"I get three meals a day, *bang* (brother)," she said.

We didn't have much time to talk; I said nothing. I bit my lip.

"*Bang*, please stop worrying about me. I will be fine."

I let her go, and she rejoined the line of marching *neary*. I watched her until she was out of sight. I never saw her again. Her labor group was moved to a place very far away. Sometime later, one of Sam Ang's friends came to our village and told me my sister had entered the *frightening* place.

I was alone in this world.

I cursed the regime all to hell.

I composed a song about Sam Ang:

Sam Ang

Thinking of the past
Makes my tears fall
Your face was so beautiful
In the middle of a quiet night
You whispered to me that you did have problems
You have problems
Karma arranged our separation
And when the morning came
You just disappeared
Leaving me alone

Whatever it takes
I hope to see you again
Life without you
Is like life without light
And full of pain
Mok Chhneang village
Why no mercy?
No mercy
Preah Andong and Cham Ro Ar
Why give me false hope?

I dream of your face all the time
I cannot forget
You are foremost in my heart
In this life I'm no longer with you
I always have sorrow
You left me for the last time, unintentionally

Oh Sam Ang
My lovely girl
This life I wish

To meet you again in the next
This life has bad karma
I wish in the next
There will be no separation
No separation
Not the way of a tree without branches
See you again without separation
See you in every life

Chapter 8

The Vietnamese took over the capital, Phnom Penh, and "liberated" our country from the Pol Pot reign of terror in January 1979, but it took me until the end of June before I escaped the Khmer Rouge for good; I was deep in the jungle, far away from the capital and the highway.[16]

One day, when *Mit* An and I were planing wood under one of the "new houses," *Mit* Chhum, an *old person*, then the head of our work group, forgot to take his radio with him when he left the work area. *Mit* An turned the radio on to listen to the broadcast of the revolution. This day happened to be January 7, 1979, the day that Vietnamese troops and their allies among elements of the Khmer Rouge took over the capital. The radio continued broadcasting and re-broadcasting the news that Phnom Penh was liberated! Pol Pot's Khmer Rouge no longer controlled the country. We immediately turned off the radio and smiled at each other, knowing that our day of liberation must be near at hand. Only the two of us knew of this. I remembered that earlier *Mit* An told me there wasn't a chance we'd ever get out of this place. But now there was a *possibility*, the possibility I could be free! My heart was pounding. Would there be fighting here? The local Khmer Rouge against the Vietnamese? Probably not, I thought. The number of soldiers here in my region was too small to fight a war. And I never saw military trucks or heavier military equipment, only the occasional cadre carrying an M16.

But it was a three to four-hour walk from Cham Ro Ar to Highway 5. I would need to reach the highway. How was I going to escape the Khmer Rouge?

---

[16] In 1978, Khmer Rouge bellicosity in the border areas with Vietnam surpassed Hanoi's threshold of tolerance. On December 22, Vietnam launched an offensive. So loathsome was the Khmer Rouge dictatorship that Vietnamese forces (historically viewed as enemies) were greeted as liberators and quickly overran most of Cambodia. Phnom Penh fell on January 7, 1979.

Within a few weeks and without a reason given, the Khmer Rouge ordered all of us to move up the mountain to Sdok Proveuk, the village our logs were transported from. Even though it was late January or early February, normally a dry time, quite a bit of rain had fallen, and the road was muddy. Masses of *new people* trudged and slipped as we made our way up through the forest toward Sdok Proveuk. There were so many of us from every village near Cham Ro Ar. *Mit* An and I kept looking at each other, but beyond exchanging glances, there was nothing we could do. Moving up toward the forest was not a good sign to us. We would much rather stay nearer the highway in order to have a better chance at escape.

It wasn't the first time I'd thought of escape. Years earlier, only a few months after we arrived in Mok Chheang, Uncle Chin Huot talked to me about escaping to Thailand. He said he knew someone who could guide us through the jungle. "We are slaves here, Seang! he said, his voice edgy and full of emotion. "Can't you see?"

He said he heard in other places "the Khmer Rouge yoked us, the *new people*, with a cow yoke to plow the ground.

"Seang, we are going to *die* here! We have to escape while we're still strong." He thought it was the best time because, back then, we were still healthy. I disagreed. Thailand was just too far away--via the highway, more than 100 kilometers, through the jungle, likely many more. There was no way we could do this. We had a large family to think about, including grandfather grandmother, and Vimol who was only 4-years-old.

"And what about Nhoan?" I asked. Ten-year-old Nhoan, his second child, had suffered polio at birth and, unable to walk, was quite heavy. Chin Huot who had four children altogether said he could wrap Nhoan up behind his back.

Not doable, I decided then, and soon afterward, Chin Huot left us for another village called Rumchek beside Highway 5. I wasn't sure how he managed this. I knew in his heart he must still have been working on a plan to escape. But those days I saw things differently. We didn't have enough cows or buffalos. What should we do? We needed rice to survive. Someone had to prepare the fields for planting. I told myself that once we had rice we'd be all right. So we had to be patient. Uncle Chin Huot never did escape.[17]

Through these many years of pain, suffering, and death, I learned one thing well: *Be patient.* And, maybe now, my time had finally come, but here we were amid a mass of people--trudging uphill--and *away* from the highway.

When we finally reached Sdok Proveuk, the Khmer Rouge told us to dig inside any dirt mound we could find so we could bury the rice. It was hard work trying to dig holes in the dirt mounds because there were so many tree roots to be cleared. We were also ordered to build more structures to accommodate all the new arrivals. (Eventually, some 400-500 persons lived here.) Not only was I still assigned to the carpenters group, but, by this time, I'd learned so much about carpentry that I'd become one of the work leaders. A Touch, the boy who'd become expert at siting rat traps in Svay Chhrum, was now under my direction, and I could spare him for other things. Sdok Pro Veuk had expansive fields of sugar cane. About 14-years-old, robust and swift, he was the best candidate to look for our supplemental food. So now his job was to gather sugar cane for me and my team.

We were very busy hiding the rice and building shelters, but, by word of mouth, the news spread that Vietnam, Cambodia's historic enemy, had invaded and was battling the Khmer Rouge. We even saw airplanes, the OV-10 Bronco, a plane we called the *"Chan Srak"* due to its appearance when seen from below. (The *chan srak* is a cylindrical, stacked food container bracketed by a rectangular metal handle; we used it to carry food to the temple.)

The Khmer Rouge fear of this plane surprised me. It wasn't a daily event, and most of the time, it was only a single plane high in the sky. Still, as soon as they heard or saw one, they scrambled to find a hiding place. I saw panic in their eyes. Maybe the plane reminded them of the war.[18] Our reaction, of course, was just the opposite. We *new people* reveled at this

---

[17] One day, about a year after he'd moved away, I saw him at the train station where I'd been sent to pick up salt. His face and legs were swollen. I didn't expect him to survive.

[18] In 1969, President Nixon and Henry Kissinger ordered a secret bombing campaign in eastern Cambodia.

sight. Not only did we watch the plane without fear, we felt deep inside that our time of liberation was near. We thought the Vietnamese must be investigating the area. By this time, we could sense that many Khmer Rouge felt unsafe among us. We noticed them trying to distance themselves. They must have feared that we, the *new people*, would side with the Vietnamese. And some of them must have feared becoming the target of our revenge. The Khmer Rouge knew that we outnumbered them, and with the fall of Phnom Penh and other major cities, they were now a minority.

When we were first moved here, the Khmer Rouge often told us, "This is the time when broken glass floats." A classic proverb said "A gourd sinks, broken glass floats." A gourd is useful to collect water (and, thus, valuable) whereas broken glass is cheap and useless. The Khmer Rouge compared themselves to broken glass. Generations of Cambodians taught their children not to be discouraged if someone did something bad to them. Someday, that bad deed would harm the doer in turn, and, thus, the gourd would no longer float. But now it seemed it was a different story. The broken glass was sinking. And we, the gourd, would likely float again.

After a few months living in Sdok Proveuk, news spread that Vietnamese troops had pushed all the way to the western border of Cambodia. The Khmer Rouge forces had retreated farther and farther into the jungle and mountains, fearful that before long the Vietnamese would find them.

Then, one night, Acha Po took me aside in his house and told me that the next morning he would move up further into the mountains, and, afterward, I would be free to go wherever I wanted. He knew that I and the rest of the *new people* would likely be safe when the Vietnamese eventually arrived. I knew this man as commanding and confident, but tonight he was uncertain, so soft-spoken, even whispery. He appeared both sad and afraid at the same time. As one of the Khmer Rouge leaders he didn't feel safe.

The next morning, in the darkness before sunup, I helped Acha Po load his belongings onto an oxcart. No one else was there, just me and his family in front of his house. I pulled both of his cows over to the front of the cart, yoked them, and tied the reins to the seat in preparation for the family's departure. Acha Po got his wife and his two boys onto the cart. I said goodbye to his wife, his son, Kra, and his younger brother. They said their goodbyes in hushed voices. I thanked Acha Po for his friendship.

Even though he was one of the Khmer Rouge leaders, he had been very good to me, and I always considered him a good person, a man I called "*bang*" (brother). He whipped one of the cows lightly, and the cart moved slowly away.

*   *   *

Now everyone, the hundreds of *new people* who'd been moved here, prepared to leave Sdok Proveuk. We all knew where the rice had been hidden. However, the Khmer Rouge order to hide the rice inside dirt mounds wasn't smart. As soon as we dug it up, we found the heat and the wetness generated had spoiled the rice. Of course, there was still some rice that wasn't spoiled. Everyone began loading the unspoiled rice and whatever vegetables they could find onto oxcarts.

Ta Nhim was another kindly, *old person* I'd met in the carpentry group. He was in his 60s and enjoyed no status in his rank the way his peers did. He was not a leader in any group. In fact, his status wasn't much different from ours, but he didn't seem to mind. He loved all of us and socialized with us as well. Like the rest of us, it seemed he just wanted to survive. Originally from Takeo Province in southwest Cambodia, he had lived here a long time and knew the area very well. We all convinced him that the best thing to do was to leave with us instead of going up into the mountains with his peers. It wasn't hard to convince him since he had no status or rank among the Khmer Rouge.

We didn't feel safe leaving Sdok Proveuk on the main road, but *Ta* Nhim knew an indirect way out. We loaded our necessities onto his cart. He rode alone. The rest of us walked behind. And so, *Ta* Nhim, another Khmer Rouge cadre with a kind heart, led my group down the mountain and through the forest toward Highway 5.

Once we descended to Svay Chhrum, there were no Khmer Rouge in sight. We reached a main road, and the number of *new people* grew as we were joined by many others also intent on reaching the highway. I passed the place where I'd drunk thirteen ladles of liquid palm sugar. I passed the "new hospital" where I'd labored carrying water. It looked to be empty. I oriented myself toward the right side of the road. I didn't know for sure where my father, mother, my sister, Sy, and Vimol, my *son*, were buried, but I somehow *knew* they were all off to my right. I walked off a little way, separating myself from the others standing at the side of the road. I clasped both my hands together at my chest in the ancient gesture of *sampeah*, lowered my head, closed my eyes, and called out to the spirits of my family--my father, mother, all my sisters, and Vimol. I gave thanks to them for saving me. It wasn't the first time I ever prayed to my parents. Every time I passed this place after leaving Svay Chhrum, I always implored their spirits to watch over me and keep me alive. Less than four years ago, I'd come here with my whole family. We loved one another and took care of one another as best we could. Now, tears streamed down my cheeks. I thanked them all. This place had been "home" for four years. This was where I'd lost all my family. Now, I was leaving this place. Alone. I felt no pity for myself, only sorrow at how my family's story had ended.

As we walked on, we passed through Cham Ro Ar. Where, before, there was the clanging of the ironsmiths' hammers, now there was only silence. It took all day for our group to reach Highway 5.

Ta Nhim was a quiet and humble villager, clearly a descendent of village farmers. He had no other family with him. As we reached Highway 5, he told us he would return to his hometown in Takeo. We thanked him for his help and kindness and wished him a safe trip home. We told him he was now as free as us. I could tell he was happy with his decision to join us. We started walking, and I watched his cart move away. Now he was free too.

* * *

My grandfather once told me that when he was young and in search of opportunity in the city, he'd walked from the southern province of Kampot to Phnom Penh, a distance of 90 miles. In those days, there were no highways. He said that on his way he'd walked through forests and over mountains and even saw wild elephants. His story of adventure and the wilderness enchanted me. And the sheer human effort? How could any person walk this far?

The distance from the western province of Pursat to Phnom Penh is 124 miles.

* * *

By this time, most of the country had already been liberated. The Khmer Rouge finally fled in shame. The Khmer Rouge had massacred millions of their own countrymen and caused the country to regress. Their revolution accomplished nothing. The scene on National Highway 5, once I set foot on it, told me the years of killing and forced labor had come to an end. The era when power was held by illiterates and sociopaths was finished. But, like others, I was now bedeviled by questions. Where do I go? Back to Prek Phnov where I was born? Phnom Penh? Or should I leave the country? Who will be the next leader of our country? Now that Vietnamese forces occupied Cambodia, were we coming under the sway of Vietnam? Throughout the history of our two countries, our two peoples had never had a good relationship. Still, I reasoned that whatever was coming next would have to be better than what I'd just gone through.

But what I witnessed on Highway 5, the scene before me, took me by surprise. The national highway teemed with people.[19] Thousands of *new people* had walked out of the jungle, villages, and labor camps where they'd slaved for years. Some were preparing to travel west and some east. Many had no idea of which way to go or even what to do next. I was sure so many of them lost their families just like I had, and this only made their decisions more difficult.

Some were planning to go back to find justice for the death of their families. I saw both the real and planned revenge *new people* were to take against the *old people*, the Khmer Rouge. I spotted a group of about eight Vietnamese soldiers. They were quite easy to spot because of their uniforms. They gave a gun to one of the *new people* who was pointing to a Khmer Rouge cadre. The new person excitedly claimed the cadre was responsible for his family's death. The Khmer Rouge took off running. He ran away from the highway. Like a rabid dog marked and chased by a crowd for destruction he ran far into the dry rice field. At the sound of a shot, I saw his body crumple to the earth. I heard people in the crowd telling whoever would listen that "the Vietnamese now give their guns to have Khmer killing Khmer--Vietnamese politics." I saw the look of

---

[19] In the Vietnamese invasion aftermath, hundreds of thousands of Khmer began long treks home and to look for family members. Many found nothing remaining of their former lives. A society anchored and identified by place, had been uprooted. The Khmer Rouge had come terrifyingly close to succeeding in their radical attempt to erase all memories of the old Cambodia. Many Khmer decided to flee to the border with Thailand though the border was a dangerous, chaotic place.

hardness on people's faces. Like me, they had seen the ones they loved suffer, starve, and die. I saw people sitting beside the road who were sharpening their knives as they prepared to return to the village to look for their family's killers.

* * *

As for me, I had no thought of going back to take Khmer Rouge lives for the terrible things they'd done to my family. I saw no point to more killing. Now it was time for peace.

Then, on the highway, a familiar face beckoned me.

"Seang, come west with me!"

Originally from Pakistan, *Ta* San had lived in Cambodia for a long time and was fluent in Khmer. We called him "*Ta* Arab" (Grandpa Arab). A tall man with a blade-like nose and a sincere smile, he hardly had to work the way we all did for the simple reason that he knew how to repair watches. He was a very lucky man, and always in demand. Every soldier, every *old person* in the village and the surrounding area knew *Ta* San. He sat and repaired watches all day long. And because watches mostly belonged to soldiers, the Khmer Rouge chief couldn't assign him any other work. I was sure he drew out his work as much as possible. And he left no doubt that he got extra food. Raising his bushy eyebrows, he would brag about the palm juice he received from his special clients. I always found him with his chipped, magnifying loupe in his right eye. Whenever he saw me, he'd remove his loupe and flash an infectious smile.

Ta San intended to march west to Thailand. He said this was our best chance to leave the country. I'd always found *Ta* San friendly and sincere, and so, without much thought, I accepted. Thailand was much nearer than Phnom Penh, and I had no family left in the country. Any chance that my youngest sister, Sam Ang, was still alive was very slim, and so I joined *Grandpa Arab*, and we started walking west toward Thailand. But after walking for a short while, I changed my mind. I was not absolutely sure that my youngest sister, Sam Ang, was dead, and I wasn't ready to give up on her yet.

I made up my mind to reverse direction and journey back to Phnom Penh with a group of friends. We were a band of about ten. I knew we would need a cart to transport rice and whatever other food we could gather along the way. Without a cart, we would starve again. Along the road, I swam across a river to look for wood to make wheels for a cart. I say "swam," but I was never a good swimmer; in fact, I don't know how to swim. (Though I was born near a river, my parents were very strict about me playing in the water.) I just took hold of a banana trunk and floated across to other bank. Once I reached the other side, I saw a scattering of many bodies, civilians, but I didn't pay much attention. I didn't believe they died from being shot or murdered; there was no sign of blood.

When I left the killing fields, I brought my hatchet with me. I loved this tool, specially made by an ironworker friend. Except when I was sleeping, it was always on my waist. Back then, I used a sharpening stone to polish it every morning. I kept it bright and shiny. (And so sharp I even used it to shave my mustache.)

With the idea of building a cart in mind, we searched for wood in an abandoned house. There, I found large, rectangular pieces of wood. They'd been arranged side by side to make a bed. In those days, typical country beds were made of very strong wood planks, at least two and a half inches thick. But with my sharp ax it didn't take me long to shape this large piece of wood into wheels. In a short while, I'd fashioned a small cart. I was a carpenter! Since none of us had any belongings, the cart was large enough to transport our rice and fruit, particularly mangos we gathered from trees along the road.

Our band set off on Highway 5, and, except to get food supplies close to the road, we stayed on the highway all the time. At night we slept on the road or in any structure we came across. It seemed as if all of Cambodia was on the move. People told one another where food could be found or where rice was stored. Telling strangers where they'd obtained food was now safe as it wouldn't deprive them of anything. People no longer feared starvation. They just carried enough food with them to last until they reached their hometown. Or the capital. Though we had to search for food, we were no longer starving. With enough food to eat, we cooked rice beside the highway.

One day, we came upon a rice storage bin abandoned by the Khmer Rouge. We took as much as we could and loaded it onto our cart. We took turns pushing and pulling the cart toward Phnom Penh. Every so often, along the way we saw dead buffalos and cows. The carcasses provided us with meat. After some days of pushing and pulling the cart along the highway, I noticed a fairly large ulcer on my right wrist. The ulcer was painless; it didn't bother me at all. From time to time, I noticed other travelers with similar skin lesions. *As soon as I get to the city, I might be able to find antibiotics somewhere.* I concluded it was likely that one of the animals we'd eaten had died of disease.

After two weeks of alternately pushing, pulling, and walking, our tired little group reached Prek Pnov, my birthplace. Now Prek Pnov was full of people again! As in old times, vendors crowded the market, but no buses were running yet. No rickety coaches with roofs piled high with luggage or merchandise. Instead of blaring bus horns and black exhaust smoke, bicycles were everywhere. And there were plenty of *romok*, bicycle-drawn carts. Of course, most people were on foot.

In Prek Pnov we stopped our cart at the first apartment on the left side of the highway, the house of my father's foster parents. Their daughter, who I called "Aunt Keu," was younger than my father. She and a few of her children were still alive. She was so happy to see me. She invited my whole group to stay with her, but everyone was eager to find his family so we parted there beside the road.[20] I said goodbye to the others, and we wished each other luck and expressed the hope we'd see each other again soon. There was sadness, but no tears. Each of us was just so happy that we could finally return home.

Aunt Keu told me about my Aunt Sok Nay. Aunt Sok Nay was the daughter of my maternal grandmother's sister. She and her family were very fortunate in that they stayed across the river from Prek Pnov during the time of the killing fields. She'd lost only one daughter to sickness. There were plenty of fish here. (After all, this was the place where people produced the noted Prek Pnov fish sauce.) Because my birthplace was only twelve kilometers from Phnom Penh, it had been liberated immediately after the capital.

Aunt Sok Nay promptly asked me to stay with her, and I readily agreed. Then she led me to the bank of the Tonle Sap and called out to her daughter, Sophal, on the other side. I burst out laughing. How could she

---

[20] During the Khmer Rouge time in power, families were often separated and sent to different places.

call out to someone on the other side of the river and expect to be heard? But her daughter heard her! She paddled her canoe across the river to pick us up. There I met Aunt Sok Nay's entire family--her husband and her six children, among them a girl nicknamed "A Srey." Srey was a distant relative. I'd known this second cousin when we were children, but took little notice of her.

In the following days, I met a few old friends of my family.

"Has anyone seen Sam Ang?"

"Has anyone seen Sam Ang?"

I put the question to everyone I met. I asked again and again, but no one had seen my sister. After a week or so, news of my arrival in Prek Pnov reached another of my aunts, Sok Kim, in Phnom Penh. She asked her son, Kong, to pick me up and bring me to her house in the city. And, one morning, 18-year-old Kong arrived on his bicycle to take me to Aunt Sok Kim's home.

I was happy to see this tall, strongly built young man with the deep voice and slight stammer, and I couldn't wait to meet the rest of his family, particularly Aunt Kim, my mother's sister. My long-range goal was to return to Phnom Penh and live there, not here. There were similarities between my family and Aunt Sok Kim's family. She had six children; I had six siblings. She and her husband owned a grocery store, like my parents. We had lived not far from each other in Phnom Penh before the war, and so I was very close to her. Her oldest son, Leng, and I attended elementary school together. We were the same age and walked to school together. Aunt Sok Kim's husband was a tall man by Cambodian standards, and I believe Leng was the tallest in the family. I learned he had died in the killing fields.

I hopped on the bike seat behind Kong and off we went. Every once in a while I offered to pedal, but Kong refused ("Don't worry, *bang*. I can do it.") The road was crowded with pedestrians and bicycles. I enjoyed the sights from the bicycle seat. It was so good to see a living society again. Except that there were fewer motorized vehicles, life didn't seem much different from the old days. Vendors hawked their wares from everywhere along the road, but there was no currency. (The Khmer Rouge had abolished it. People used Thai currency instead.) Cassette players along the road broadcast old Khmer pop music. I hadn't heard this music for so long, and now to hear some of my favorite songs again brought me joy.

This was the same road our family followed when we were trucked out of the city years earlier. When Kong pedaled past the village at Kilometer 6, I saw the Chhroy Changva Bridge on my left. Collapsed at the middle, its purpose destroyed, it lay like something dead. Below was the riverbank where father and I used to wait for the boat to Kean Klaing, his birthplace. Beyond and to the right was the French Embassy. I saw no activity there. Next, Kong pedaled passed the French community; there were no foreigners to be seen. The mammoth Catholic cathedral that used to stand next to my medical school was gone. The Khmer Rouge had razed this structure. My medical school building practically leaped out at me. It had been painted red. The entire building![21] I asked Kong to stop. I just *had* to go inside. Education meant so much to me. I walked up the front steps and went inside. It was empty. I stood there in silence. I opened the large door that led to the amphitheater and found no one. I was alone in one of the few high-ceiled structures in Cambodia. I stood inside for a while and just let memories return. I stood on a spot facing the wall where our exam results were always posted. Every time, as soon as test results were posted, a thick crowd of students formed at this wall. If your test score was high, your name would appear at the top of the list for all to see. If you failed the exam, your name would be at the bottom.

Finally, I'd seen enough. I descended the large stairway in the front of the school to where Kong waited. From here we continued along Monivong Boulevard all the way to Chbar Ampeuv where my aunt lived.

I was overjoyed to see Aunt Sok Kim. Always a very emotional person, my aunt quickly ran out of words when she saw me. She cried. Finally, through her tears she was able to say, "You stay with me. Don't worry. I have plenty to feed you." I was overwhelmed by her generosity. Her own apartment was small, but she had a small houseboat on the river (actually a raft).[22] I had never been in a *floating house* before. I lay down on the

---

[21] These days, the school is known by its nickname: "The Red Medical School."

[22] Aunt Sok Kim and her family were displaced to Kratié along the Mekong River during the Pol Pot years. After the fall of the Khmer Rouge, they decided to build a raft to float the family to Phnom Penh. The whole family cut bamboo and tied it together to make a raft. They found a small, abandoned hut next to the river, lifted it onto and secured it to the raft. Then, they let the daytime current carry them toward Phnom Penh.

bamboo floor and just let my mind drift. The cool breeze and the sound of the waves slapping at the riverbank and the expansive view to the other side of the river made this place seem like heaven. I couldn't believe that only a few weeks earlier I was *out there*, deep in the mountains, and today I was free in a *floating house* with time to enjoy the view of my city.

The next day, and in the days that followed, I pedaled my aunt's bicycle around the city to observe what other damage the Khmer Rouge had done. One structure that captured my attention was the National Bank. It lay in ruins. The Khmer Rouge had blown it up.[23]

It took some time, but I eventually found my old home. It had been more than four years since I'd seen it. The house stood empty, like so many others. No one lived in it now. The back doors of all three floors were open. I dashed first to my room to look for my photo albums. What I had hoped was to find my pictures, the ones I'd left behind when my family was forced out. I missed those pictures so much. More than four years ago, when we were displaced, I'd left them here because I thought we would be back soon, and I didn't want to run the risk of ruining them. The windows of my room were also open. The floor was marked with water stains, and my medical books lay strewn across the floor. All the pages were stuck together. Ruined, all. Then I walked through the entire building, every floor. The windows were open. The building could have been looted, but I couldn't tell for sure. Nothing was left. All my childhood pictures were gone.

My moped was gone too.

* * *

Aunt Sok Kim gave me a picture of myself taken when I was a teenager. Aunt Sok Nay gave me a picture of my mother. I treasured them both--the photos and my aunts.

After some days of pedaling about the capital, I thought I'd better find a job, so as not to burden Aunt Sok Kim, but she advised me I needn't hurry because she could afford to take care of me. She cautioned me to be extra careful since the country was now run by a Khmer government

---

[23] The National Library, repository of Khmer cultural treasures, had been turned into a pigsty by the Khmer Rouge.

that was "propped up" by the Vietnamese. She suggested I wait until the country was more stable before going back to work.

I found out that my old classmate, Mithona Nhok, was the chief surgeon in Calmette Hospital, the formerly private and most famous French hospital in the capital. One day, I stopped by to visit him. He welcomed me to his office where I enjoyed my first taste of ice cream in four years. (It was exceedingly good. And *cold*.) When I complained my teeth hurt, Mithona laughed at me for being a "country bumpkin." He also gave me an antibiotic to treat the skin infection I'd developed from eating infected buffalo meat. Mithona suggested I join him by applying for a job through the Minister of Health. I completed the application, but then, remembering Aunt Sok Kim's words, I held it. But, as time went on, I felt uncomfortable having Aunt Sok Kim support me, and, after about a month, I decided it was time to be independent again. I submitted the application and was selected for a position in a new clinic/hospital, the January 7th Hospital, a former Chinese hospital. The clinic, an aging former high school, was located across the street from the hospital.

When she heard I was going to work as a doctor, Aunt Sok Kim took me to a tailor and generously bought me many pairs of new clothes. The colors were so flashy and bright: yellow, orange, even teal! At first, I felt uncomfortable wearing them. I had been wearing black pajama-like clothes for so long, and had only two pairs at that.

I moved out of my aunt's place and into a huge house along with a couple of friends that another former medical student had located. It was a three-story house belonging to a former doctor of the January 7th Hospital. It was within walking distance of this hospital where we worked.

At the clinic, I joined Doctor Tan Tek Sreng[24] who had been two years ahead of me in medical school. He'd begun working there a few months earlier. I was so happy to be back to my former career, but at the same time I felt uneasy about working as a doctor without any retraining or returning to medical school.

I longed to hold a medical book again. One day, I and a housemate, Khoy You Deth,[25] went out to the Russian hospital to look for medical

---

[24] Dr. Tan Tek Sreng is now a gastroenterologist in Phnom Penh.
[25] Dr. Khoy You Deth is currently a pharmacist in Paris.

books. The hospital, one of the largest in the city, sat abandoned. I was quite familiar with this place as was Deth, whose mother lived nearby. We found a few old medical books in the hospital's library. It felt so good to hold medical textbooks again. We rushed back to the house and immediately started reading. At the January 7th Hospital, I got to meet a few former professors: Dr. Thai Va, Dr. Nuth Savoeun, Dr. Sao Sokhon, and a few other colleagues such as Dr. Yit Sinnara.[26] My job was to provide adult care in the clinic and conduct rounds in the hospital.

There were so few of us that we were essentially on call every day. I was to receive no income from my work; my compensation was rice, corn and meat. It was at this time that my relationship with Srey, who had become my girlfriend, became more serious. Before I began working at the January 7th Hospital, I'd spent a good deal of time with Aunt Sok Nay's family across the river from Prek Pnov. Making use of my carpentry skills, I helped Srey's father build a new two-story house. The roof was made of palm leaf panels that Srey and her mother had sewn in preparation. As I worked to secure the leaves on the roof, Srey would pass additional panels up to me. Working alongside the family, I got to know Srey better. Sometimes, I fetched water from the river with a yoke and buckets. (This task reminded me of the job I used to do in the killing fields.) During my work break, she boiled corn she had planted.

Eventually, Srey asked me if I could find her a job in the city, and I did. I got her a job as a nurse in the clinic. Dr. Sreng and I trained her. Despite having no prior nursing training or health-related education, she performed her job well, and it pleased me to see her form good relationships with other staff.

Each day, the clinic work challenged us. All my friends and I were so happy to work there though none of us had received any further training or formal education. We just worked. And worked. There were so few of us and so many patients. We worked under the Medical Director, Dr. Nuth Savoeun, a pediatrician and our former professor.

Our manager was a woman who'd been a long-time member of the Vietnamese-supported government of Heng Samrin. She was chiefly responsible for rice, corn and meat reimbursement, but she also oversaw

---

[26] Dr. Yit Sinnara is now a well-known pediatrician in Phnom Penh.

medication dispensing protocols. To my knowledge, she had no medical background. Still, she told us how many pills we should dispense to each patient per visit based on (I can only suppose) the storage level of that particular medication. I could see this resulted in inadequate therapeutic regimens for certain diseases such as infections. A patient, for example, might require a seven-day course of therapy, but receive only three days of therapy. As time went on, I grew uncomfortable with this, especially after I learned she had no medical background. But the country's previous health care system had been destroyed by the Khmer Rouge and needed to be rebuilt; a new government was being constituted. This was a new regime, and I was not about to cause any disruption.

Chapter 9

One day while I was working in the clinic with Dr. Sreng, a young boy asked me for antibiotics. This boy wasn't sick himself, but he said he needed antibiotics for a relative. I told him I couldn't give him more than a three-day supply (per the hospital manager's edict), but all he needed to do was return in three days, and I would give him more. The young boy, who I'll call "Ohn," said he couldn't. He said he was leaving with another person that coming Sunday for the Thai border and wouldn't be back for at least a month.

I asked Ohn about his trip. How would he travel to the border? He told me he'd be traveling by bicycle. I was very interested. His comment came on top of other talk I'd been hearing, and it set me to thinking. By this time, a number of small political movements were springing up on the outskirts of the capital, particularly at the village known as Kilometer 6 where people were talking of forming a political group to oust the Vietnamese-propped government. Supposedly, this movement was even stronger at a camp on the Thai-Cambodian border known as "Camp 007." I knew of a former medical student, Pok Saradat, my Uncle Sy Nay Heng's classmate, who was known to be a high-ranking officer in Camp 007. Both Pok Saradat and my Uncle Sy Nay Heng had joined the Cambodian military's Medical Corps years before, and that's how I knew him. I'd assisted Pok Saradat in a few surgeries when I volunteered at Monivong Hospital as a medical student. Pok Saradat had joined an opposition political party, the Khmer People's National Liberation Front. The KPNLF, a political front organized in opposition to the Vietnamese-installed government in Phnom Penh, ran Camp 007.

Earlier, my housemate friend Deth had departed for the border. Two of his brothers lived in Paris. His mother still had assets enough to finance travel to the border. They paid someone to help and went by truck. Boldara, another of my classmates, later married Deth, and her sister, Kun, had gone with them. At the time, I had no intention of leaving Cambodia. I knew no one in the outside world. And I had no money. But now, here was someone, Ohn, to guide me free of charge. So when Ohn told me about his trip, I was more than a little interested.

* * *

That same week, I decided. Knowing that the current regime was associated with Vietnam, I reasoned it was better for me to leave the country. Two other friends of mine, Ngo Ngam Song and Nhean Chamnam, had already left Phnom Penh for the border. I strongly believed that, in the end, the various Khmer movements along the border would triumph. And there was something else that gave me pause. I was told there was a possibility that we, as health care practitioners, would be sent to Vietnam and Russia to complete our medical training. I was hungry to further my medical training, but the idea of going to Russia distressed me, and I certainly did not want to go to Vietnam. I'd just narrowly escaped one communist movement; I wanted to avoid communist regimes altogether. Too, I was unhappy working under a hospital manager who, though she had no medical training, was responsible for all the medical policies.

I'd left the killing fields alive; I was quite sure I would survive anything. This was different from how I felt when I labored in the killing fields. During the *starving season*, I was very humble. Challenging work meant nothing to me. I remember when I was starving, I told myself that when peace returned, I'd look for a small place to stay, out on a farm. I'd build a small hut and plant potatoes around the house so I would *never* starve. My life would be complete. As a city dweller, a medical student, I'd never had such thoughts. I remembered when the *starving season* reached a peak, how just a small bite of potato or rice tasted so sweet. If I had potatoes, I didn't need anything else. It was quite a powerful feeling at the time, and I thought I would stick to this plan for as long as I lived, but the thought didn't last.

Of my family of twenty-four persons, I was the sole survivor. Everyone in my family died: my parents, my five sisters, my grandparents, my mother's siblings, my uncle's family, and my sister's family. I'd left the killing fields alone. I was certain now that I'd lost every member of my family, including Sam Ang.

Whatever decision I made, it affected just me. I had nothing to lose. *But now, there was Srey.*

I'd lived a lonely life for quite some time, and now I had someone who cared deeply for me. To have Srey next to me at all times was wonderful. But there was a cost. If she was to go with me, join her life to mine, then I had to take good care of her and protect her as best I could.

Again, without a second thought, I told my girlfriend, Srey, that I was ready to make a try for the border. I told her I was looking for a better life, and she could join me. I *had* to go, I said. I told her that wherever I went, I would survive. Srey said she was determined to be with me for better or worse. The next day, I borrowed a scooter from a friend at the hospital and drove Srey to Prek Pnov to request her parents' permission to make a try for the border.

I sat, waiting on the moped for Srey on the side of the road in Prek Pnov. So that she could speak openly with her mother, I hadn't accompanied Srey when she crossed the river to her parents' house. Of the two parents, her mother was likely the main decision-maker. Young girls at that time did not say much about a relationship. In Cambodian culture, so much was left unspoken. In general, mothers made decisions for their daughters. If her mother had not allowed it, there was no chance Srey would be leaving with me. When Srey finally crossed the river and returned to where I waited, she told me her mother had given her permission. Her mother had wished her luck and had even given her a gold necklace with a pendant of the Buddha. I was elated, but not really that surprised because, by that time, I knew in my heart her mother believed in me. Over the past months, working beside them, I'd come to know the whole family through the way Srey and her parents interacted with me. Srey got on the back of the borrowed moped and we drove back to Phnom Penh that day in a daze of joy. I went to my aunt, Sok Kim, and told her of my plan.

* * *

On Sunday November 18, 1979, the day we'd chosen to leave for the border, all of the medical staff was scheduled to visit Tuol Sleng, the high school that the Khmer Rouge had transformed into a torture center. I forged a patient discharge letter for use by Srey stating that she was released from the January 7th Hospital and was to return home to Svay Poh in the western province of Battambang. I had access to the hospital forms so it wasn't that difficult to generate the letter. This was not the first time I forged a letter;

I did this once when I was in the killing fields to get myself being admitted to the "hospital" in an attempt to get closer to the hospital kitchen. There is an old Khmer saying: *Plov veach kom boh bong, plov na trong kom deu hong.* It means "Do not forsake the crooked road; never walk the straight road." Back then, choosing to walk the crooked road saved my life.

On the letter, I used my sister's name, "Sam Ang," instead of Srey's. I signed it with the letter "K" representing my friend's name, Khoy You Deth, who had left Phnom Penh a few weeks earlier.

Ministry of Health   Peoples Republic of Cambodia
And Social Affairs   Independence Peace Prosperity
7 January Hospital
Number: 0774

Authorized Hospital Discharge Letter

Name: Srey Sam Ang   Sex: Female   Age: 22
Address: Khum Svay Poh   Srok Sangke
Province: Battambang
Date of Admission: Day 17th   Month: 8   Year: 1979
Date of Discharge: Day 17th   Month: 11   Year: 1979
Has been doing well and is allowed to leave the hospital and return to her home.
This letter expires on the 25th of November 1979
Phnom Penh Day 17th   Month: 11   Year: 1979
Commission of hospital 7 January

I chose an expiration date that was a week after our actual departure, just in case anything unexpected delayed us.

* * *

There wasn't much for Srey and I to do in preparation. We had so few belongings. The night before we were to leave, I said goodbye to Aunt Sok Kim. She wished me good luck and said she would pray for me to have a safe trip. Finding out that my mother's sister was still alive had been a blessing to me. I had found her and stayed with her for less than two months, and now I'd decided to leave the country. The truth of this saddened me, but, true to her Buddhist nature and love for me, Aunt Sok Kim understood my reasoning. She herself wasn't sure it was a good idea for me to begin working with this new government. She'd cautioned me about taking a job too soon. She, too, just felt sad that we would no longer be together. My departure was difficult for both of us. At what must have been a great personal cost to her, she provided Srey and me with a new bicycle for our journey. Some of the clothes she had the tailor make for me were still new and had never been worn. I'd given these to A Touch a few days earlier. According to the hospital discharge letter I'd forged, Srey and I were supposedly returning to our hometown in Battambang so carrying new clothes wouldn't really fit with the story we were prepared to tell.

The night before our departure, I couldn't sleep much. I hadn't told anyone else of our plan. No one at the shared house knew that I planned to leave, not even my partner, Dr. Sreng. I kept thinking about how unpredictable and dangerous a journey we were about to take. We had no money. Our only material asset was the gold necklace with the Buddha pendant Srey's mother had given her.

Before I knew it, morning had broken. Srey and I woke early.

I'd arranged for Ohn to meet us at our workplace, the Chinese hospital. It was within walking distance, about two blocks from the house. I didn't want to meet at the house because I guarded my plan closely. I didn't want anyone to know I was leaving. By 5 am, Srey and I reached the stoplight at the intersection. Standing next to Ohn was *Ta* San, the Parkistani-born, watch-repair man, the same *Grandfather Arab* I'd followed west immediately after escaping the killing fields. To my great surprise, it was *Ta* San who was to accompany us and the boy, Ohn. I soon learned from *Ta* San that months before when we'd parted on Highway 5, he had continued on his journey to Thailand. He managed to reach Thailand, but was ordered to return to Cambodia by the Thai authorities. He had to make his way back through the mountain of Dang Rek, a trail that would eventually claim thousands of lives from sickness and starvation, as well as from violent death in minefields. Hearing that made me so glad I hadn't gone with him then.

But the situation was different now. I already heard there were refugee camps along the border, and a few of them were supervised by the United Nations High Commissioner for Refugees (UNHCR). I thought there was a good possibility I could make it through to a refugee camp in Thailand. And if I couldn't, then I could stay on the border and join a revolutionary group that was working on seizing our country back from Vietnam. I could join the forces there as a medical staffer and could contribute to the country, especially if I were working with Pok Saradat as a surgeon.

It was time for us to depart for Thailand on two bicycles, just the four of us--Srey, myself, *Ta* San, and the young boy, Ohn. We stared out at Highway 5. The border with Thailand lay more than 250 miles away.

* * *

The new bicycle my aunt provided us had a metal frame with a seat mounted over the rear tire. Srey took her place on the rear seat, and we left Phnom Penh under a clear sky. Four of us on two bikes--off we went. The weather was warm. The hospital letter I'd forged was tucked in my pocket. We pedaled off with nothing but the clothes we were wearing, an extra set of clothes for each of us in a bag, the *krama* (the traditional Khmer scarf), and the necklace Srey's mother had given her. That was how Srey and I started life together. In Cambodia in the 60's and 70's a song by Joan Baez was very popular--"500 miles." I used to listen to it. *"Not a shirt on my back, not a penny to my name."* It was so true that day--not a penny to my name. But the decision was final. I had no hesitation. It was Sunday, November 18, 1979.

Ohn had traveled Highway 5 a number of times so he knew places we could stop to rest and where we could sleep along the road. He had come prepared with his rice pot and rice. He said our goal should be to pedal 100 kilometers a day with the idea of arriving at a city each day before dark. Our plan was to travel only in the daytime, starting at dawn. We started pedaling, riding our bicycles parallel to the River Tonle Sap, the ribbon of mocha water to our right. The first 40 kilometers of pedaling was especially painful for me. I had never ridden a bicycle very far. My body ached and my legs kept cramping. More than once, I had to ask Srey to relieve me, but she was just too small; she couldn't do it.

From time to time, we encountered a checkpoint on the highway. The soldiers manning them didn't interrogate us at all; they simply asked us where we were headed. As Ohn had been through this so many times in the past, he usually responded for all of us. I didn't even have to make use of my hospital letter since we all appeared to be what we, in fact, were--travelers from the city to the countryside.

Our first destination was Kampong Chhnang, about 56 miles from Phnom Penh. Kampong Chhnang means "riverbank cooking pot." This town was well known for its terra cotta water urns, cooking pots, and portable stoves, the kind with three legs to support the pot and an extension bed for firewood. It was difficult pedaling in the area of Kampong Chhnang, too, as the road turned steeply uphill for long stretches that seemed even longer when pedaling with a person on the back. I'd never pedaled a bicycle this far in my life. Though I'd recovered from starvation, my leg muscles were still not that strong. Thankfully, *Ta* San, Grandfather Arab, was willing and able to help. When I ran out of strength, he offered to pedal for me, and Ohn would carry Srey. I owed much to *Ta* San and Ohn for allowing me to rest when I got fatigued.

My worry at the time was the possibility of a flat tire. In those days our lives were simplified by the limited resources available. I dared not hope for the luxury of a spare tire or tools to fix a flat. I felt so grateful to Aunt Sok Kim for giving us the means, the bicycle, to travel. The majority of Cambodians lived a life of poverty. What they possessed, they cherished and passed on for generations. If a person lost a pair of slippers, he went barefoot. If a bowl was chipped, it would be used until it broke. If a *krama* was torn, it was patched until it was completely worn out. Life was lived this way. That's why Cambodians are always praying for everything, from the birth of a child to the passing of an exam, looking for a job, moving into a new house, travelling, farming, or entering the hospital. Cambodians are always praying. That's what I worried about--a spare tire.

Cambodians are a people who live life without a spare.

In Kampong Chhnang we passed the night in a vendor's shed. Ohn had done this many times before. Vendors usually lived in houses behind their own sheds. As he'd done on numerous past trips, Ohn simply walked into the main house and requested a place to stay for the night. We didn't even have to pay the vendors.

Pursat, about 60 miles from Kampong Chhnang, was our next destination. Riding was much easier here. By now, I'd become used to pedaling, and the highway cut across a flat landscape. This was the same road, Highway 5, my family and I were trucked to the dirt road that led us to the village during the Khmer Rouge era. When we reached this area, I thought of all of my family members who had lost their lives in the labor camp. Once again, I gave thanks for my survival. Here, again, Ohn sought out a local vendor, and we spent the night in a shed.

In the evening, we cooked rice over a fire beside the highway. As I squatted before the fire and stirred the pot, I thought to the time I brought my mother a can of rice (in a concentrated milk can) I'd stolen from the hospital kitchen. Mother's head was shaved to rid her of lice. Her face was swollen and round like the moon. Her eyelids swelled outwardly, almost closing her eyes. Her lower lip had swelled and hung downward leaving her lower gums exposed. Her legs were swollen grotesquely with fluid. In contrast, her chest had sunk like the chest of a tuberculosis sufferer. I stared at her, stunned at how much she had changed. I tried not to cry, but I felt so much pity for her that somehow my tears just flowed. I had an unmistakable feeling that she could read my mind and understood what I felt. But how could she tell me of her sorrows, when she knew I had my own to bear? She turned her back to me and busied herself starting the fire to cook the rice I'd brought.

I said "goodbye," but she suggested I stay so we could have dinner together. "Mom, you need the rice; don't worry about me. In fact, I have to go back before sunset," I insisted.

"It won't take long," she said and as she pushed the wood deeper under the covered pot. "Tonight we will have cooked rice instead of porridge."

"But I'm not hungry, mom," I lied, and got ready to leave.

"Listen, son. As you can tell, I won't live much longer. Have you forgotten how your father died?"

"No, I haven't forgotten."

To please her, I stayed, and we ate rice together. She was sent to the "hospital" a couple of days later.

* * *

The next day we covered another 65 miles to Battambang. Now we were nearing our final destination although as we neared Battambang, our supply of rice ran low. Ohn told us how we could get more. A vendor who sold rice would cut a few links from our only asset, the gold necklace Srey's mother had given her. The vendor weighed it with his jewelry scale and then gave us the equivalent value in rice. (All the vendors seemed to use jewelry scales since the only other currency was the Thai *baht*.)[27]

Here, again, we spent the night in a vendor's shed alongside Highway 5. We only had about 65 more miles to go before we reached Poipet, the last town before the Thai border.

How my life had changed. I was now free to make my own decisions. I'd been making decisions on own since my parents had passed, but that was within the restrictive boundaries imposed by the Khmer Rouge. Now there were no boundaries. And now, I had a lifelong partner--Srey. It had only been a brief five months, but our relationship was strong. I had no time to think of much else but to survive this journey. I had no backup plan. If this plan failed, I'd need to come up with another one, but for now I was only looking forward.

As we got closer to our destination we noticed the soldiers manning the checkpoints were Vietnamese, but I could speak enough Vietnamese to get by. I just told the soldiers my wife and I were returning to our hometown.

Finally, after five days of pedaling, we arrived in Poipet, the last town before we would attempt entry into Camp 007. Neither of the bicycles had even gotten a flat tire.

The only thing separating Poipet from Camp 007 was the forest, and its location had made Poipet a haven for smugglers. The town was alive with people, and its open market bustled. While we were strolling through the market, I happened to spot *Mit* Sam (the former law student who'd worked as a secretary for *Ta* Kdam). This was an incredible coincidence, and he was as surprised as I was. I hadn't seen *Mit* Sam since leaving Mok Chhneang more than two years before. (First, *Ta* San and now, *Mit* Sam!)

Mit Sam had been living here with his wife and sister-in-law for some time, and they all appeared happy and healthy. Sam worked as a "*neak rotpun*," a smuggler, buying merchandise from Thailand and then

---

[27] We still have this necklace though it's now quite short. Once, our daughter, Sakara, took it to her elementary school for "show and tell."

reselling it in Cambodia.[28] He said he made a good living by traveling into the camp, buying merchandise, and returning to his village to sell it. Meanwhile, as we chatted with *Mit* Sam, *Ta* San and Ohn wandered off in search of someone to guide us to Camp 007. We spoke for only a short while, less than an hour. *Mit* Sam and his wife invited us to stay with them if we would like to. They were good friends, and I could tell their welcome was sincere.

After only a short while, *Ta* San and Ohn returned with word of success; they'd located someone to guide us through the forest. (But this was to cost us another segment of the necklace.) We thanked *Mit* Sam and his wife for their generosity and politely refused their offer. My goal was to make it to a refugee camp.[29] We parted there in the busy market. It was the last time I was to see *Mit* Sam.

It was in Poipet that we finally left Highway 5. From here on, we would travel at night, a dangerous walk through the forest to reach Camp 007, an unofficial refugee camp (not run by the UN) situated on the Cambodian side of the border. This camp was controlled by the KPNLF (Khmer People's National Liberation Front), a political front organized in opposition to the Vietnamese-installed government in Phnom Penh.[30]

This winding road through the forest had claimed many lives in the past. We were told the area was riddled with mines left over from years of war. In the Poipet market, I had asked Srey to stay behind with *Mit* Sam's family while I went on ahead with Ohn and *Ta* San to gauge how safe it was. But Srey was adamant. She said if it must be, we will die together.

---

[28] A wild array of black marketeers and other traders sprouted up in and around border camps. Corruption was rife along the border, and black market trade in food and other essentials was widespread. Gold, hidden away by many Cambodians during the Khmer Rouge era, was one of the most common forms of currency.

[29] Throughout 1979, thousands of Cambodians fled to the Thai border. Barred from entering the country by the Thai military, a vast number accumulated in several makeshift camps along the ill-defined border. Many were starving, suffering from malaria, or otherwise in poor health. Conditions were poor; most of those who settled in the camps lived in squalor and lacked access to basic services.

[30] Far from being a safe haven, many border camps were subject to attack as conflict continued between remnants of the Khmer Rouge and Vietnamese forces. Refugees were caught in the middle. A different Khmer military faction controlled each of the border camps, and battles between them were frequent.

There was no way I could convince her to stay. So, once night fell, we found ourselves amid a long line of people walking through the unknown forest. It was so dark, and the line of walking people was so long I couldn't see to the front or the back of it. No longer able to ride the bicycle, we just dragged it along with us. I had no clue who was leading whom. Each of us just blindly followed the person in front of him. I didn't know who the guide was or even what he looked like. We were instructed to closely follow the person in front of us and warned not to wander off the path, a path that, at times, narrowed so much that only one person could pass along it. I had to carry the bicycle off the ground. As we hiked single file through the forest dark, we could hear the roaring of wild animals-- wolves, I thought, judging by the sound--but it didn't bother me; what I feared most were the silent, unseen killers that lurked underfoot; I feared stepping on a mine. I repeatedly cautioned Srey to carefully follow in my footsteps.

Finally, after walking through the dark all night, we came to a checkpoint--the last checkpoint. Soldiers manned it. They were Khmer dressed in military uniforms, the KPNLF. This could change everything. It was at this checkpoint that armed men would either accept us or deny us entry into Camp 007.

I looked at Srey. Her cheeks were so red and smooth. She was only 22-years-old. We'd passed at least five checkpoints by this time. I'd confidently talked my way through them, but at this final checkpoint, a real fear gripped me. I was so afraid.

What would I do if these fighters said "yes" to only one of us?

* * *

Aside from "praying" to pass my school exams, I was never the kind of person who really *believed* in prayer. Living through the *starving season*, I saw so many people who truly believed, including my grandparents, but they all perished. Still, here I was, praying for both of us that day. Srey had no way of knowing this. I never told her. Maybe I was too embarrassed. In any case, we were both admitted into Camp 007.[31]

The camp was a sea of humanity. People lived in small thatched huts.

---

[31] Camp 007 was a large refugee camp with an area of about four square kilometers, flat land occupied by approximately 60,000 refugees.

They were thrown up everywhere. You could even buy one if you had gold, or *baht*, the Thai currency. Outside the area where people built their huts, there were plenty of tall trees. There were no toilets. For privacy, you had to go off the compound a little bit. But seeking privacy might not be safe. For our own safety, we chose not to wander around very much.

At first, the sight of so many Khmer soldiers wearing American military uniforms reassured me. Most commonly, they carried M16s though some had AK-47s. However, after our long journey, seeing how people lived in the camp, I was disappointed. The look of life in 007 unnerved me. I could see there was definitely a distinction between the people and the military. Most of the people here had nothing to do with the military or politics. They were here either looking for food provided by the International Committee of the Red Cross (ICRC) or to work in the black market.

I wasn't sure what was next, but I did meet three friends from medical school--my former classmates, Nhean Chamnam, Long, and Ngo Ngam Song. *Bang* (brother) Song was two years ahead of me in medical school. I knew *Bang* Song well because he had been a classmate of my role model, and uncle, Nay Heng, who had drowned shortly before the Khmer Rouge seized power. Chamnam and Song had left Phnom Penh long before us, and I never thought I'd meet them here in 007. I had no idea of what I was going to do next, but my parents' spirit seemed to be with me. I felt they'd guided me to this unexpected rendezvous with Song and Chamnam. I learned Chamnam had traveled here by truck with her sister, Channan, and her nephew, Kal.[32] Chamnam had a hut and invited us to stay with her.

I wasn't sure what I was going to do. I was told it wasn't that easy to meet Pok Saradat, the soldier/doctor I thought I could depend on. And now, I wasn't even sure I wanted to meet him. Aside from the fact that he was Sy Nay Heng's friend, I knew very little of him. I'd assisted him in a few surgeries in Monivong Hospital, but I didn't see any hospital or operating room near where we stayed in this camp. And too many people in need of help.

Only the day before, a holding center called Khao I Dang (KID) had opened. I learned this was in Thai territory and run by the United

---

[32] Dr. Song is now a pediatrician in Long Beach, California. Nhean Chamnam is an artist and lives in Paris.

Nations High Commissioner for Refugees (UNHCR).[33] But to qualify to be transported there you had to be related to a sick person. In other words, if a family member was sick, the entire family would be transported to KID.

Bang Song knew of a family with a sick child. Song, who spoke both French and English, was assisting this family. They were very thankful. To add all of us as the patient's family seemed a small kindness the father could do for Song. At the same time, the family now had someone to assist them in their upcoming journey to KID. So, somehow, Song managed to get us included as part of that child's family. That same afternoon, we were all transported by bus to KID. I was so happy because I wasn't sure how we would survive in Camp 007. There was no job for me here, and I hadn't come all this way to become a smuggler. And Srey and I had no resources except for the now-shortened necklace with the Buddha amulet.

We departed the afternoon of the day of our arrival. I was so happy not to have to spend the night in 007. Here, we parted from Ohn and *Ta* San. Before we boarded the bus that would take us across the border to Thailand, I donated my bicycle to Ohn, the boy who had done so much to help us get this far.

For the past five days Srey had sat on the back of my bike. Now I was so happy to be sitting next to her on a bus headed across the border to Khao I Dang in Thailand. Maybe we were on this bus ride across the border because, like Cambodians so often do, I had prayed.

Or, maybe, once again, I was just lucky.

---

[33] Throughout most of 1979, the Thai government refused offers of humanitarian assistance from the United Nations for Cambodians at the border. As the border situation grew more desperate, international pressure and the offer of substantial amounts of money convinced the Thai government to allow UNICEF and ICRC to begin a formal border relief operation. The government reversed its policy of barring Cambodians from entering the country and implemented an "open door" policy. Khao I Dang opened on November 21, 1979, several kilometers inside of Thailand, just north of the border town Aranyaprathet.

Chapter 10

I breathed a little easier once our bus rolled through the gate to Khao I Dang (KID), the sprawling camp thrown up beside the small mountain that gave it its name. KID was located seven miles inside the kingdom of Thailand. We arrived on November 22, 1979; the camp had opened only the day before.

We stepped down off the bus and looked around. Within just seven miles, the world had changed. The very air and even the dazzling sky itself for some reason looked different. I knew that my life was changing too.

Everywhere we looked we saw foreigners, and the sight brought me comfort. I started to believe in luck again. For the past four years my life had been filled with tragedy, starvation, death, and unknowns. A long chain of events had brought me to this camp. I felt this was what was meant to be. I *belonged* here. Some of the first things I noticed were the multiple hospital wards that lined both sides of the camp entrance, each with a name posted at its entryway. Nothing could describe how I felt at that moment. I thought back to the career I 'd begun more than four years ago in Phnom Penh's medical school. The desire to be a doctor burned in me again. Any thought of building a small hut in the Cambodian countryside and planting potatoes was now dead.

Srey and I, Bang Song, and my friend, Chamnam, were all assigned to section 2. Srey and I were given a "T number," a tracing number, signifying we were officially admitted into the camp, and we were photographed. It was the first time I had my picture taken since April 1975. In the picture, I smiled broadly.

* * *

Every day, I saw truck after truck piled high with bamboo roll into the camp. Soon the whole camp was transformed into a bamboo city. I had never seen anything quite like this before. Camp 007 was just a clearing in the jungle. Khao I Dang was a world away from this. KID was very well organized. Food was distributed to the refugees via a representative in each section. The volunteer section representatives were chosen by the section members. The food, mainly rice and salty fish, was supplied by the United Nations High Commissioner for Refugees (UNHCR). Distribution was both orderly and peaceful. Having just survived the killing fields, everyone was so happy to receive even the simplest fare.

Life here was simple. And safe. The water was clean, too--no longer milky as it had been in the Khmer Rouge labor camp. Large, square water tanks had been installed to supply the refugees. All we had to do was to walk to the tank area and collect it in plastic containers we were provided. Young children, the majority of them shirtless and some naked, liked to gather around these tanks. They laughed and chased each other around the tanks. They climbed atop the tanks and sat with their legs dangling. Some stood up and danced. They behaved just like kids. Some even fashioned a yoke to carry water back to their hut as people do in the village. It was the kind of joyful scene I hadn't witnessed for the past four years.

Our camp neighbors, the Prak Sin family, lived in a hut across from us on the other side of the walkway. Prak Sin was selected to be our representative section. He made sure we received bamboo and thatch, the necessary materials to build our hut. Refugees were instructed to build their huts along a continuous row, leaving narrow walkways to provide access. Some people just slept on the ground; but as for me, the carpenter, a hut was only the beginning. I used leftover bamboo to build a small bed, just large enough for Srey and me. Our completed hut was only about four feet tall so we had to bend down to enter, but we had no complaints; we were grateful to the UNHCR for proving us supplies.

Water buffalo searched for grass in the fields surrounding Khao I Dang. It was harvest season so the landscape here was parched and dust was everywhere. Most days, in an effort to keep the dust down, trucks spread water onto the camp road. Traffic into the camp was heavy. Besides countless truckloads of bamboo and thatch, numerous Red Cross cars, trucks, pickups, and motorcycles rolled in. And lots of people. Refugees from Cambodia continued to enter and the camp population swelled quickly.[34]

Camp construction was rapid and constant. The peaceful environment, coupled with the presence of so many foreigners, made me feel great. The Cambodian people were *living* again, just like in the old days--before the Khmer Rouge. Soon, camp markets sprang to life. People sold food and cassette tapes of Khmer pop music. Men could be seen playing volleyball. Laughing children with homemade toys played everywhere. Barbers set up shops. People built larger compounds to serve as community centers. Cultural arts, English, and Khmer classes were started. Some of the refugees even began a school for classical Cambodian dance. Talented individuals worked to preserve Khmer culture that had almost been lost in the killing fields. Camp life was just like living in a small town with the freedom to walk around--except there was a camp boundary made of barbed wire and patrolled by Thai soldiers.

One day, Chamnam's sister bought a cucumber from the market and invited us to share dinner with her. I watched her peel the cucumber's outer skin. Then she slowly began to make meticulous, decorative cuts so that the cucumber would be pleasing to the eye. I watched as she finished the fine cuts and then carefully arranged the slices in the center and around the rim of the plate. Before the war, I'd seen my mother prepare cucumbers like this, but that was years ago, in times of peace.

I laughed at her. "I can't believe you survived the labor camps."

She smiled back, knowing I'd been watching her. "We're living in a different time now. We eat because it tastes good, not because we're hungry."

She was right. The subject of food no longer *consumed* us. When we greeted each other, we no longer asked, "How many cans of rice are shared by ten persons where you live? Real or watery rice?"

---

[34] Set amid rice fields, the Khao I Dang relocation center population would eventually reach 160,000 persons. For a time, more Cambodians lived in KID than in any Cambodian city outside of Phnom Penh.

Hunger didn't own us anymore. Still, I was careful not to eat too many slices.

* * *

The Khao I Dang camp hospital was made up of ten thatch and bamboo wards, each run by a different country or agency. Hospital wards were built on both sides of the camp entrance. On my second day in camp, I started walking from the camp entrance, passing ward after ward, paying close attention to the sign posted on each--German, French, Japanese, Thai Red Cross, Catholic Ward, and so on. Finally, toward the end of the complex, I saw a sign that read:

Ward I
Acute Adult Medicine
Staffed by
Kampuchean Volunteers
And the
American Refugee Committee

I walked inside and (in halting English) asked to be a volunteer. My choice of the ARC ward was no coincidence. I had searched for an American medical ward in this new camp even before I had time to finish building my hut. I was interested in only *one* ward. My goal was to go to America.

ARC Ward One was an Adult Acute Medicine ward. Like the others, it was built of bamboo and thatch. The ward was one long room with a gravel floor and a high ceiling to provide ventilation. A large oxygen tank sat at the front entrance. The ward had 110 beds set in multiple rows. Plastic string was strung high along the head of each bed to hold a patient's chart, IV fluid, or even an x-ray. Families were allowed to stay with the patients so it wasn't uncommon to see multiple family members, including children, in one bed. The hospital provided three meals a day to each patient and his family. Most of the time, this was a meal of rice, fish, and vegetables.

Srey and I, and my friend, Chamnam, all began working on the ARC ward. I was quite familiar with the majority of the diseases here. Patients suffered from malnourishment and pneumonia and tropical infectious diseases such as cholera, dysentery, malaria, and tuberculosis. Many were quite sick. Meningitis was somewhat prevalent, and, later, when the ARC Ward was designated the "Meningitis Ward," many patients died.

The very first group of volunteer doctors and nurses I worked with on Ward One was from Minnesota. These amiable professionals were willing to help in any way they could. It buoyed me to see them care for their Cambodian patients the way all humans are supposed to be treated. These Westerners also took the time to train our Khmer staff. They showed the Khmer how to give injections, change dressings, and to pass medications to patients. They built an atmosphere of camaraderie with us. I noticed the American staff also played with the young children. Sometimes, they brought us food from a town outside the camp. After finishing their medical rounds, they even took the time to teach English to us. I remember one session when a doctor taught us how to tell time in English. We all just gathered around the doctor, out in the open, at the front of the ward. The day was hot and humid. We had no desks or chairs. We stood on the dusty, hard-packed earth, but the lesson was friendly and quite fun.

It was on the ARC Ward one day that I again met Dr. Haing Ngor. We'd known each other in Phnom Penh before the Khmer Rouge seized power. In those days, he'd worked as a doctor at Monivong Hospital, the same hospital I worked in as a medical student volunteer.[35] As soon as he spotted me, the first words out of his mouth were "I thought you died in the labor camp."

"I thought *you* didn't survive," I quickly replied. Later, as I explored the sprawling camp, I was to find a few medical school classmates who'd also managed to get here. Some of them worked on the German surgical ward located just opposite ours. Bang Song worked in the outpatient department. Long worked with the French group.

* * *

Nearly all the refugees at Khao I Dang had been victims of the Khmer Rouge, whether they'd been students like me, professionals, merchants,

---

[35] Dr. Haing Ngor was in a different category than most of the refugees. He lived outside the camp and came to work with the ARC. Haing later won the Best Supporting Actor Oscar for his role in *"The Killing Fields."*

small vendors, or farmers. A separate camp had been set up for Khmer Rouge cadre and their families, many of whom had also fled to Thailand. From time to time, a Khmer Rouge cadre was identified at KID. Very shortly, camp authorities would send that person to the separate camp for fear that someone would take vengeance on him.

By word of mouth, I learned that a Khmer Rouge cadre named *Ta* Chhen was in Khao I Dang. This man had been responsible for all the rice, sugar, and produce storage in Cham Ro Ar. He determined which village received food stores and in what quantity. Though I'd crossed paths with him a few times, I'd been careful to avoid this mean "Chief of Commerce." While his stores of food were plentiful, we starved.

One day, I found myself seeking him out at this hut in Khao I Dang.

As soon as he laid eyes on me, I knew he remembered who I was. The boastful Khmer Rouge chief grew silent. Gone was all his yelling. I politely told him the reason I'd taken the time to find him.

"Look at your situation now. Look at the concern and love the foreigners show for the Khmer. Your heart is Khmer. You were born Khmer, and yet you treated Khmer as slaves. Many here know you are Khmer Rouge, yet we treat you no differently from the rest of us."

I turned and walked out of his hut and left him to his thoughts. Stepping out into blazing sunlight, I felt very good that I'd had a chance to say this to him.

* * *

Since the collapse of the Khmer Rouge regime of terror at the beginning of the year, international news outlets had begun reporting on the plight of the Cambodian people. The sight of hundreds of thousands of refugees, country people who normally do not move from their rural villages, fleeing to the safety of neighboring Thailand stunned the world. A number of journalists and media reporters converged on Khao I Dang.[36]

Working shifts around the clock, we began to develop a very good

---

[36] One of the media outlets who visited KID was Iowa Public Television. Their crew filmed the volunteer medical staffers as well as the camp. I happened to be one of the interviewees in their film called "Don't Forget the Khmer" though I didn't see the film until much later.

relationship with the American volunteer staff. Wendy Wornham, for example, was a medical student when she worked in KID. When I told her that Srey and I never had a wedding ceremony, she carried a watermelon into our hut one day and offered us a celebration that we had missed. As friends do, other staffers took pictures of us and gave us prints as souvenirs. Since I'd lost all the pictures of my past, I restarted my past by cherishing these photos.

These medical personnel treated me as if I were one of their team members. They allowed me to conduct rounds on the ward. They shared their medical textbooks with me. Though my English was poor at the time, I could read and understand medical books well enough because of the similarity of medical and technical terms. I'd never known these people before, but, in a very short time, we formed a strong bond. I came to feel that many of these volunteers were now my family. My first real friendship with the American people had begun.

One of the physicians who worked with us on the ARC ward was Dr. Daniel Susott, a tall, angular man about my age who'd graduated from the University of Hawaii's School of Medicine. (Later, he was to become medical director of the whole camp.) Daniel told me Hawaii would be an ideal place for me and Srey to live. I could even attend medical school there, he said. Despite my poor English skills, he wrote letters to the Dean of the medical school, and asked many other physicians to write letters of recommendation to the school.

Now that I had an official tracing number and support and encouragement from the ARC members, how could I not feel happy? Still, I couldn't help but wonder how long we would be in this camp. And, for that matter, how long would the camp even remain open? Srey had become pregnant with our first child, and with each extra day we spent in Khao I Dang my anxiety about our yet-to-be-born child grew. I had few concerns about Srey's health or about a delivery in camp. I trusted the obstetricians here. There was a maternity ward near the ARC ward, and if a cesarean section became necessary, the operating room was well equipped to deal with an emergency, and the surgeons were from developed countries. I would no longer have to deal with illiterate *child doctors*, but I worried about our child's future if we had to remain for years. And still, sometimes before dawn, came the low rumble of artillery from the direction of the border seven miles away. Thai? Vietnamese? Who knew?

Still, having survived the killing fields, I remained optimistic. We were well off compared to the majority of refugees. The ARC staff gave me clothes, brought me extra food from the town outside camp, gave me a set of medical scrubs and a stethoscope, and I even got to work alongside them on the medical ward. I didn't even have to worry over getting sick. I realized how lucky I was compared to the majority of refugees. *Don't complain about anything*, I told myself.

* * *

One day as I was returning to my hut at the end of working my shift on the ward, I spotted a tall American wearing a gray hat and surrounded by refugees. I made my way through the curious crowd and found out this man had a notebook containing the addresses of many Cambodians in the U.S. I glanced at his notebook and discovered the address of Srey's uncle in Georgia. Yet another lucky opportunity! I rushed back to our hut to tell Srey. I hurriedly wrote a letter to her uncle. An ARC team member mailed it for us, but, as the days wore on, we received no answer.

A short time after this, I was given another address in France--this time of my aunt, Ee Chin. (She was the sister-in-law of my uncle Chin Huot, my mother's brother). I had no intention of going to France, but I thought I should remain open to the idea of emigrating to another country; there was no guarantee I would be going to America. Also, I knew and spoke more French than English, so dealing with language might be less challenging for me in France. Ee Chin also had a sister, Ee Eang, who happened to be in the refugee camp too. I wrote Ee Chin a letter asking for her help. But because she was a distant relative, I didn't expect she would help me. To my surprise, Ee Chin answered my letter, and before I knew it she had completed all the paperwork necessary for Srey and me to emigrate to France! I didn't know what to say. At last, we could see a real chance to leave the refugee camp.

As it turned out, Srey's uncle had moved from Georgia to California, and the post office forwarded our letter to him--Dr. Sin Meng Srun,

Professor of Forestry in Humboldt University.[37] Later, we received Dr. Srun's paperwork to serve as our sponsor. Both Dr. Sin Meng Srun and his wife, Bo Sin, were also very kind to us by sending us $50.00 a month while we were in Khao I Dang. I'll never forget their generosity.

The acceptance of my wife and me to America by Dr. Sin eased the burden on Daniel somewhat. Without a sponsor, the chance to leaving the camp was very low. With a sponsor, the chance was much better, but the waiting period could still be quite long. In the meantime, Dan had convinced me that going to Hawaii would be a better choice for us than California. I might even have a chance to attend medical school there and resume my life, a life that had been stolen by the Khmer Rouge more than four years before. It looked to me that settling in Hawaii would give me a better chance of returning to school. Daniel began communicating with an agency in Hawaii called "Hawaii Refugee Organization" (HRO). We trusted that Daniel would get us to America eventually.

On the ARC Ward I also met Bob Richard, a registered nurse and hospital administrator from Iowa who always had words of encouragement. He told me he, too, had faith in Daniel. On his last day, the day Bob departed KID for home, I walked with him toward the entrance of the camp. He hugged me tight and told me not to worry. "Daniel will get you out of here," he said. Bob gave me his phone number and told me not to forget to call him collect when I reached Hawaii. (Then he had to explain the meaning of a "collect" phone call.)

I was very impressed with the medical skills of yet another physician, Dr. Bill Haggard, a family practitioner. I once watched him lance a peritonsillar abscess of Dr. Sam, another Khmer physician who worked on Ward One. The German team had suggested that Dr. Sam needed to be placed under general anesthesia before having his abscess drained in order to prevent aspiration. But Dr. Bill pointed out that general anesthesia itself carried significant risks, and suggested local anesthesia as the better choice. I watched as he incised the abscess with confidence. No complications

---

[37] In California, the Sin family thought I could help them manage a donut shop. They planned to buy a donut shop for us to operate. This way, they thought I wouldn't have to look for jobs in America. At the time, their generous offer puzzled me. Back then, I didn't know what a donut shop was.

resulted. Dr. Bill had a twin brother, and before he left KID he gave me a gold coin, explaining that his twin had a matching coin. He stressed that it was a gold coin so if I needed to, I could trade it for currency. He said he carried this coin to bring him luck and hoped it would bring me luck too.

I much appreciated the work and enjoyed the friendship of the other Khmer and ARC members. First was the Minnesota team, then the Iowa team, and, lastly, the Chicago team. Each group stayed for about two months, at the end of which its members would return home. The bond I formed with them was deep. I felt as if they were part of my family. Every time an ARC group left us, I cried.

* * *

When the time finally arrived for Srey and me to leave Khao I Dang for the Chonburi Transit Camp, the ARC team hosted a farewell party for us. We had spent seven months here, and we were so happy to leave, knowing that we were taking another step closer to America.

The ARC ward was packed with patients and the hut reserved for medical staff was too small, so we all gathered in the open space outside the ward. Dr. Sam brought his wife and three children. Dr. Haing Ngor joined in too. Strings of flowers decorated our necks. Balloons hung suspended from plastic string above our heads. Cameras clicked. So many pictures were taken. Moving often from place to place in order to prepare for a photo proved difficult for Srey who appeared to be in full term by this time, but she kept her smile.

All of our patients' families, many of them children, formed a circle around us. Some were shirtless and probably unaware of what was occurring. We couldn't blame the children for crowding into the photos. How often did they have their picture taken?

A crowd of refugee onlookers surrounded us, and I was quite sure all of them wished they could share our good fortune. We were in a different situation than other Khmers because of the assistance we received from Dan.

Three days later, as we sat on an idling bus outside the camp gate, some of the ARC staff came to wave goodbye. From my seat at the window, I looked out over their heads at the sprawling camp. When we departed Khao I Dang, so many refugees were still there, waiting. I could read the anxiety on their faces. I couldn't believe my luck. I whispered, *"Lea heuy* (goodbye) Khao I Dang. *Lea heuy,* bamboo city."

After our arrival at the Chonburi Transit Camp, we didn't work. For the most part, we just waited to be called to Bangkok for the all-important embassy interview. Many ARC friends came to visit us during our stay here. One day, Daniel brought my wife a soft mattress to comfort Srey.

Lumphini would be the next and final stage of our stay in Thailand. Lumphini is in Bangkok, the capital. The atmosphere here was different from both KID and Chonburi because all of the refugees housed here were expected to leave Thailand for a third country. We were even allowed to temporarily leave the camp if friends or relatives were granted a permit from the camp officials. Once, a group of ARC friends took Srey and me out to dine in the metropolis of Bangkok. (For the first time, I tasted pizza.) We also got the chance to visit Bangkok's zoo with many members of the ARC team. But my mind wasn't on the food, the zoo, or the vast megalopolis that was Bangkok. I was thinking only of our upcoming journey to America. A friend had once reminded me that if your plane didn't leave the ground, you weren't leaving the camp. And life in the killing fields had taught me to expect the unexpected. So I didn't want to feel overjoyed that we'd made it as far as Lumphini.

Finally, the day arrived when Daniel asked me to prepare for an interview at the American Embassy. I shaved and grabbed a clean, white T-shirt and tucked it nicely into my trousers. I combed my hair and waited for Dan to pick me up. When Dan arrived, he politely, diplomatically, let me know I needed to change clothes. I learned then not to wear a T-shirt to an interview.

Srey had become pregnant while we were in KID, and by the time we'd been relocated to the Lumphini Holding Center she was already at term. Our first child could be born at any time. Srey had never been examined by a Thai doctor. Dan, so caring, didn't want our first baby to be born in this place--under these conditions. If the interviewer should ask about my wife's last menstrual period, he advised, I should respond with a date consistent with a pregnancy of about six months. Dan had also written a note to the International Center for Environmental Management stating that on July 27, 1980 he had examined my wife in Chonburi, and her pregnancy had not advanced more than six months.

I did as Dan advised. The interview must have gone well--we were cleared to depart Bangkok on August 27, 1980.

By the date of our departure, Srey was obviously at term, but, with the "evidence" of Dan's letter, we weren't challenged when it came time to board the plane.

At the airport, Dr. Daniel Susott, Chris Feld, Debbie Tate, and Dr. Haing Ngor were among the friends who came to see us off. At last, after all the farewells and good wishes, we took our seats on the plane. I waited patiently to see if the plane was going to move. If those wheels didn't leave the ground, I wasn't going to America. When the plane finally roared down the runway and lifted into the air, I smiled and whispered to myself, "I was chosen." There were more than 160,000 refugees in Khao I Dang, and I was among the chosen ones to come to America, a realization that overwhelmed me. I looked forward to challenging myself to survive in America. I would do whatever I needed to do. All that mattered now were our two seats on that plane flying across the Pacific Ocean. The bicycle odyssey from Phnom Penh, the dangerous trek across the border, life in Khao I Dang, holding centers and transit camps, the submission of applications to third countries, the embassy interview--none of these events mattered now. Once the plane's wheels left the ground, I took a very deep breath and grabbed Srey's hand. It was my first time on an airplane.

I was flying now.

Epilogue

The people of Tonga have a saying: *The greatest wealth is feeling gratitude.* This is so, and I am wealthy beyond measure.

Dan's parents, the Susotts, greeted us upon our arrival in Honolulu. Dan's father, a colonel in the Air Force, and his mother, a pediatrician, drove us to the office of the Hawaii Refugee Organization. Dan's mother assisted Srey who, fatigued after the long flight and full-term pregnancy, lay on the office floor to rest. With the help of a social worker, the Hawaii Refugee Organization first found us a temporary place to stay and then an apartment in Honolulu. The sight of coconut trees along the Ala Wai canal behind my apartment made me feel at home.

My first impression of America was very positive. Everywhere we went on Oahu, the streets were clean and well paved. Street corners included ramps to allow the handicapped to cross the streets. Special parking permits allowed them easier access to their destinations. For people with impaired vision, an audible alert at the crosswalk announced when it is safe to walk. I'd been curious about the thing called a "freeway system." How could people build streets that you could just keep driving along? It was beyond my understanding, but once I saw them--"Ah ha," I said. *Pretty clever, these Americans.* And, in a major change from my country, people respected traffic laws. Here, pedestrians were treated well, even when they jaywalked.

Rather than pushing each other to get to the head of the line, Americans lined up in single file. The park next to our apartment had exercise benches to encourage children and adults to exercise. Department stores were open and inviting. Customers were free to look at anything they wanted without anyone following or watching them. We found that in supermarkets we could just pick up the produce and examine it.

What's good about America is that the majority of people respect the law. When an ambulance passes through with a siren, drivers move to the side of the road no matter how rushed they might be.

* * *

For the first 18 months in Honolulu we existed on welfare. The monthly support we received was adequate, but we had to be very careful about our spending. Food stamps helped us get by, but I felt uncomfortable using them. I felt everyone's eyes on me, that they could tell I was receiving government support. I preferred not spending money on things we didn't need such as a telephone. In Cambodia, our family didn't have a telephone. And here, we had nobody to call. I wanted to decline it, but was advised it was important for the welfare department to contact me, and so we had to spend $13.00 each month for a telephone.

As we neared the end of the 18-month period of public assistance, the social worker informed me I needed to look for work. I tried numerous places, but had no luck. Applying for a job at Burger King, I was asked if I had a high school diploma. I was turned down for another job opening for a security guard, perhaps because I'm a small-framed Asian. Eventually, I asked my social worker if I could be allowed to stay in school. The answer was no. So, after 18 months, we lost our government support. Looking back, I was grateful for public assistance. Without it I don't know how we would have survived.

I decided the best course was for me and our new family was to attend school and so my wife had to find work. Srey started by cleaning houses, but she later found a better job in a French bakery. On weekends, I also worked--delivering hair shampoo and lotion door-to-door in high-rise apartments. My boss dropped me off at the lobby, and I ran in circles on each floor to hang a sample lotion pack on each doorknob.

Srey and I seized on any job that allowed us to work from home. Once, a friend of Daniel's gave us a job stringing leis. I even went to Waikiki to sell them.

We were poor back then, but in time I managed to save enough money to buy a camera, something I'd been dreaming of for a long time. The first thing I did was to take lots and lots of pictures. As soon as I printed a roll, I organized the photos in albums. I had lost nearly everything from my previous life in Cambodia, and old family photos were some of the things I missed most. I was determined not to allow this to happen to our children.

What I constantly worried over was how we would begin a new life here. I knew that without a good command of English, getting into medical school would remain only a dream. Once a friend of Daniel's asked me what I wanted to do, and after I told him, he said it would be very difficult to get into medical school with my English background. Weak as I was in English, I could read his unmistakable body language. What he really meant was that, based on my age and poor English, there was *no* chance for me to get into medical school. I didn't let it bother me though. That fall I attended two adult high schools and earned my GED. Then I registered for classes in the community college. Transferring to the University of Hawaii in the fall of 1981, I applied to the Imi Ho' ōla Program, the fast-paced, very competitive pre-med program for Pacific islanders. I couldn't meet the English requirement the first year, and, later, when I gained admission I found I lagged far behind the other students, both in English and the basic sciences. Students faced endless quizzes, each with only five questions. Two missed questions meant a grade of "C." After a host of Ds and Fs, I feared my dream of medical school would never be realized. Once, I went to see Dr. Benjamin Young, the Associate Dean, and, thinking my education was over, cried my eyes out. I also wrote a letter to an ARC doctor I knew from the Khao I Dang camp in Thailand and poured out my concerns. I told him I'd been too optimistic about getting an education in America. (In his reply, he advised me to go to the beach and relax.)

My classmates could tell I was near drowning, but I refused to give up. I had a wife and baby to care for. I bought a tape recorder and recorded every single biology and embryology lecture. Typically, a one-hour lecture took me about four hours to transcribe, and then I studied another two hours to understand it. I searched a Cambodian-English dictionary as often as I did the medical textbooks. Saturdays and Sundays ceased to exist for me.

One day the girlfriend of one of my classmates came into the class in the middle of the lecture to surprise him with a birthday cake. (Our Imi class was quite small--about 25 students.) Everyone began singing "Happy Birthday." All of a sudden, I felt tears rolling down my cheeks. I tried to hold them back and excused myself from class. When I was growing up, the Khmer didn't celebrate birthdays. I'd never had a birthday party. This celebration was reserved for the king or monks, only the most esteemed in society, not laypersons. The majority of Cambodians, like farmers, didn't even remember the date they were born. At the particular moment that my med school classmates were singing "Happy Birthday," I began to feel so lonely.

I repeated Imi Ho' ōla, and, with the help of my old notes and much-improved English, I was finally accepted into the John A. Burns School of Medicine at the University of Hawaii in 1984. It was only then that I started to wear the University of Hawaii School of Medicine T-shirt. I'd had the shirt for a long time, but never worn it because I feared the embarrassment if I didn't make into the school.

Once I was admitted, medical school proved a great challenge for me. My cultural background had not prepared me for American university life. In Cambodia, we were raised to be humble and respectful--not courageous or daring. As students we lacked the confidence in conversational engagement or to pose questions. We were taught to listen and obey. I remember once being asked to present an anatomy lecture to my med school classmates. My hands shook, and my speech became incomprehensible. None of my peers seemed to react negatively to my speech; perhaps they pitied me or it might just be their Aloha spirit.

I had a very busy life, but I was happy with what I was achieving. When Srey began work, I cared for Sakona in the morning, feeding him breakfast, and then taking him out to the day care center. After classes I came back to pick him up from day care, fed him dinner, and waited until Srey returned home before dashing off to the library. This was my daily routine. More than once, my classmates teased me about riding a bicycle with a baby seat over the rear wheel. They often invited me to join them for baseball and basketball games, but I never did. It wasn't the time for me to have fun, but I didn't mind: I had plenty of food to fill my stomach, I was in medical school, and I was free.

When I graduated from medical school in 1988, Bob Richard, the registered nurse and hospital administrator from Iowa I'd met at the ARC Ward at Khao I Dang, was there to help me on with my robe. Srey and a host of friends presented me with leis as is the custom at a Hawaiian graduation. Other ARC staffers, nurses like Noy Stevaux and Chris Feld, joined in the celebration. Aunt Bo Chum and her husband and a host of other friends attended. Of course, Dan Susott brought his smile to the day. Well-wishers' flower leis piled up so thickly on my neck that my face was barely visible. I was so happy, though I wished I could have shared my success story with my parents. Still, I much enjoyed my special day--my first graduation party.

* * *

Sakona, our first son, was born ten days after our arrival to Honolulu. I was so happy he was born an American citizen that I named him "Free Bird." It took me a while to come up with this name. And, to this day I haven't encountered many Cambodians who carry this name. I'm proud of myself to have chosen it. He loved to be independent, a boy quite mature for his age. As he grew, he filled his summers with work, whether as a paperboy or baseball empire, a knife seller or a worker in a tomato factory. After high school he attended the University of California San Diego. Before he left San Diego, Sakona sent me a gift. It was a picture of him on the beach. The accompanying note read:

> Happy Birthday Dad!!! I hope that this gift reaches you in time. This shot was taken May 29th at the foot of Scripps Pier, one of San Diego's premier beach breaks. I chose this particular picture and frame because it seemed fitting for where I am in my life today. I am leaving San Diego for good and it's been a great seven years. I will definitely miss it. However, I know that I am off to bigger and better things. Medical school, clinical rotations, and residencies are all on the near horizon. I hope that in the years that I've been away, I have done enough to make you proud. As you continue to watch my life unfold, you should realize that it is really your life's work that has set the table for mine. Therefore, whenever you look at this photograph of me, you should see yourself in it.

I was so happy knowing that he was off to a good start. I didn't foresee him driving an ambulance for a living (after college Sakona spent two years with an ambulance company). I was so happy that day to hear that he was heading to medical school. After all, I always see myself in my children. Sakona is now an Emergency Medicine Physician. He currently serves as Medical Director of the Emergency Department at Kaweah Delta Medical Center in Visalia, California. He and his physician wife, Elizabeth Ngo, have three children.

Kosal, our second son, had his mind set on becoming a doctor since he was in high school. He graduated from Stanford University in 2008 before moving on to attend the John A. Burns School of Medicine at the University of Hawaii, the same school I had attended. One day he wrote me this:

> Living by myself here in Hawaii and facing the challenge of medical school here always reminds me of how hard it must have been for you and mom while you were in medical school, adjusting to a new country, different language, and raising Sakona and me. Years ago I was with Sakona when he was still in college and he asked me if I thought we were somehow gifted. I told him no, we were just lucky to have been raised in a safe place, with food on the table, and parents that always stressed education above all else. Sakona very much agreed. As we all get older we start to appreciate how precious it is to be able to come together as family. It's sad to think that this will become increasingly difficult to do. But one thing I look forward to is the years ahead when you and mom can instead come visit us in our homes and watch us raise our own families.

Kosal graduated from USC's Internal Medicine residency program in 2016. He is currently is at the University of California Davis for Pulmonology critical care fellowship program. He is married to Tammie Nguyen, a pediatrician in Roseville, California.[38]

---

[38] While still a student in Modesto High School, Kosal founded "Panthers Against Landmines," a nonprofit organization that strives to promote peace and security by raising funds to remove landmines in Asia, Africa, and the Middle East.

Sakara, our youngest, is blessed. She grew up at the time when we could accommodate her busy schedule that included, among others-- jump rope, piano lessons, basketball, swimming, water polo, and orchestra. She is the one that I have spent most of my time with.

One day, during her sophomore year, I took her to the Bridge, the Asian community center in Modesto, and, after examining the Cambodian two-stringed instrument called the "Tro," she expressed an interest in learning traditional Cambodian songs. Since then, she has become quite accomplished. I am so proud of her for being interested in our Khmer culture.

Sakara is the second of our children to attend Stanford. While she was in her second year there, she asked me if I had any documents relating to my experience in the Khao I Dang camp. I gave her a tape titled "Do Not Forget the Khmer." After viewing the tape, she expressed her reactions in an essay:

> His voice sounded vaguely familiar. Distorted a little, but there was something about it. I listened to the voice-over harder, paying less attention to the PBS video footage and more to the narrator's voice. His heavily accented English described the painful work day in the Khmer Rouge labor camps: 'We begin work at four or five o'clock in the a.m., and we stop working at eleven and we begin to work afternoon from one o'clock p.m. and during the night we work also from seven p.m. to ten or sometime eleven p.m.,' the voice said in halting and hesitant English. Abruptly, the documentary video flipped from rare footage of the Cambodian agrarian camps to a familiar face--one I've seen a number of times in family photo albums.
>
> *Ba*? (Dad?)
> There he was. Talking to a journalist with an accent stronger than he now has, but unmistakably his. *Ba's* face is younger--smoother skin, longer, blacker hair, but the same frown lines. It was surreal to see video footage of him, twenty something-years-old in the UNHCR refugee

camp in Thailand, fresh out of three years and eight months in one of the most barbaric social revolutions in history. *Ba's* interview finished and the PBS documentary continued sharing footage of the refugee camp and the status of the Khmer people. I watched especially closely to see if I could catch him in the background somewhere. He showed up five more times, in person and in voice-overs.

'All my family. I have twenty-four members. And all were dead because they didn't have enough rice to eat,' he said.

'Most people feel very sad. Like me. I don't know how is my future. How will I stay? Because in here, we cannot stay for many years.'

This dad I was watching didn't know what the future held for him. He didn't know that he would befriend an American doctor who would help him get into the John A. Burns Medical School in Hawaii. He didn't know he would graduate and establish himself as a county family physician in Modesto CA. Nor did he know his son would become an emergency medicine doctor or that his other son would attend the same medical school as he. He didn't know his future daughter would be quoting the words he spoke to the journalist as a Khmer refugee in 1980 Thailand.

Sakara received a grant from Stanford to go to Cambodia to work with an NGO assembling a display celebrating the achievements of various human peace activists in Cambodia. Her book, "Resilience: Celebrating the Lives of Cambodian Peace Builders," was printed in 2012.

On April 17, 2015, Sakara wrote on her Facebook page:

40 years ago today Dad was 24 years old, two years from graduating from medical school and in the same place I am. Today is the anniversary of the Khmer Rouge

takeover, and tomorrow is the day he was evacuated to a Pursat labor camp. I guess it can be cliché to imagine myself in my parents' shoes, but today especially I think about it. I wanted to write and share that April 17ᵗʰ is important to me. I am grateful, humble, and can only hope to be as strong as the 24-year-old medical student he was.

Sakara attended medical school at Western University of Health Sciences and got accepted to Internal Medicine Residency Program at Santa Clara Valley Medical Center in 2017.

Many years ago, when I lived in Hawaii, I became acquainted with the story of Dr. Arthur Guyton. Dr. Guyton graduated from Harvard Medical School. Though he'd pursued his dream to become a surgeon, he finally entered the teaching profession, eventually earning renown for his "Textbook of Medical Physiology." But what struck me most about Dr. Guyton's story was that he was father to ten children, and all of them became medical doctors. All ten of them! This story has stuck in my head through these many years. There is a saying in Cambodia, "the leaves never fall too far from the tree's trunk," and I am so glad and proud that my three children are doctors--just like I am.

* * *

A few ordinary words about some other extraordinary people:

My girlfriend, Srey, who rode on the back of my bicycle from Phnom Penh to the Thai border, and then insisted on hiking with me through a dark, dangerous forest, is now my wife of more than 35 years and the mother of our three children. She has also become a registered nurse in Modesto, California.

Dr. Daniel Susott who I worked with on ARC Ward One has changed our lives and the lives of our children. Without him, Sakona, our first son, would not have been born an American citizen ten days after we arrived in Hawaii. Dr. Susott continues his volunteer work.

My mother's sister, Aunt Sok Kim, who sheltered and cared for me in Phnom Penh, trusted in me and my dreams, and, at great personal cost, provided me a bicycle in 1979, is now reunited with her three children in San Jose, California. Her son, Darith Khay, also attended the John A. Burns School of Medicine at the University of Hawaii, the same school I had attended. Dr. Darith Khay is currently practicing Family Medicine in San Jose. Aunt Sok Kim retains her charm, bubbly personality, and quick laugh. She truly lives her *Buddha nature*, and I will never forget her generosity.

A Touch, the young teen who helped me set out rat traps and searched out sugar cane to feed our carpentry group still lives in the Cambodian countryside. In 2008 I visited him at his village house. He is now married with children and serves as the police chief in his village. I had hoped this position would help him live at least an average life in Cambodia, but, sadly, he is as poor as others in his village. When I saw him last, he was in need of landfill to fill in the swamp behind his house. I was happy to help him expand his land so that he could build a larger home for his family, for which he expressed his gratitude.

A Da, the handicapped girl who not only ignored my stealing from the "hospital" kitchen rice pot, but even stood lookout at the kitchen door, still lives in Cambodia. Whenever I make one of my return trips to Cambodia, I always find time to visit A Da. The last time I met with her was in December 2014 at which time she invited me to return for the wedding of her only daughter.

If you saw the movie "The Killing Fields," you saw the performance of my friend, Dr. Haing Ngor. We attended the same medical school in Phnom Penh, the only one in the country, and later we met unexpectedly in the Khao I Dang refugee camp in Thailand. Haing had also worked in the capital's Monivong Hospital. I never dreamed my friend would become an actor. He had no background in acting, and yet performed his role well enough to win the Oscar for Best Supporting Actor. Haing once told reporters that he was not acting in the movie because the events depicted in the film were real. He even quipped that he'd attended the "Khmer Rouge School of Acting."

Mit An, the carpenter who worked with me roofing houses in Cham Ro Ar, is still alive. I met him again on one of my return trips to Cambodia. We lunched together in Phnom Penh.

Looking back on my life's story, if I hadn't encountered my friends, Song and Chamnam, at the desperate, chaotic place that was Camp 007, Srey and I might have been trapped in a lonely and precarious life there. This fortuitous meeting changed my life. We all remain in contact to this day.

In spite of the passage of many years, for some reason I cling to the hope that my younger sister, Sam Ang, for whom I fashioned a pair of sandals, still lives. When Aunt Sok Kim still lived in Phnom Penh, I asked her to travel to Cham Ro Ar to search for Sam Ang. I also posted ads in the Phnom Penh newspaper. Following one of these posts, someone claimed Sam Ang was alive and even provided an address in Paris; however, the report turned out to be untrue.

CPSIA information can be obtained
at www.ICGtesting.com
Printed in the USA
BVOW03s1949071217
501828BV00005B/136/P